TOGETHER WE LEAD

How Principals & Instructional Coaches Team Up for Lasting Impact

Michelle Marrillia | Brittany Mozingo | Rebecca Nicolas

FOREWORD BY WILLIAM M. FERRITER

Solution Tree | Press

555 North Morton Street
Bloomington, IN 47404
800.733.6786 (toll free) / 812.336.7700
FAX: 812.336.7790

email: info@SolutionTree.com
SolutionTree.com

Visit **go.SolutionTree.com/leadership** to download the free reproducibles in this book.

Printed in the United States of America

The mark of responsible forestry

Library of Congress Cataloging-in-Publication Data

Names: Marrillia, Michelle author | Mozingo, Brittany author | Nicolas, Rebecca author
Title: Together we lead : how principals and instructional coaches team up for lasting impact / Michelle Marrillia, Brittany Mozingo, Rebecca Nicolas.
Description: Bloomington, IN : Solution Tree Press, [2026] | Includes bibliographical references and index.
Identifiers: LCCN 2025031703 (print) | LCCN 2025031704 (ebook) | ISBN 9798893740516 paperback | ISBN 9798893740523 ebook
Subjects: LCSH: Educational leadership--United States | School administrators--Professional relationships--United States
Classification: LCC LB2805 .M28425 2026 (print) | LCC LB2805 (ebook)
LC record available at https://lccn.loc.gov/2025031703
LC ebook record available at https://lccn.loc.gov/2025031704

Solution Tree
Cameron L. Rains, CEO
Edmund M. Ackerman, President

Solution Tree Press
Publisher: Kendra Slayton
Associate Publisher: Todd Brakke
Acquisitions Director: Hilary Goff
Editorial Director: Laurel Hecker
Art Director: Rian Anderson
Managing Editor: Sarah Ludwig
Copy Chief: Jessi Finn
Production Editor: Paige Duke
Proofreader: Jessica Starr
Text and Cover Designer: Abigail Bowen
Content Development Specialist: Amy Rubenstein
Associate Editor: Elijah Oates
Editorial Assistant: Madison Chartier

ACKNOWLEDGMENTS

This book was built from years of collaborating in the lobbies of professional learning conferences, over lunch tables during cafeteria duty, and in the hallway for our after-the-meeting meetings to figure out the best move for our students and our school. We have been blessed to work together for over a decade as a school-based team and, more recently, as Solution Tree associates, learning from one another, our incredibly talented faculty and staff, and our colleagues at Solution Tree. Our partnership has provided us with opportunities to learn and grow in this work.

We are so grateful for the encouragement of Claudia Wheatley, queen of the subtle and not-so-subtle nudge, and the gentle direction of Amy Rubenstein, the first person who reassured us that we had something important to say about coaches and principals. We are also so grateful for Paige Duke, who helped us frame our experiences in a way that might inform the experiences of others. This book would not exist without your guidance and expertise.

We would like to acknowledge the people in our lives who are not technically educators but who have patiently listened to us vent, theorize, and create solutions for both the challenges of our daily work and the writing of this book. We spent hours away from our families as we vetted drafts and configured the book's tools. We are grateful for your patience and grace in picking up the slack at home and giving us the gift of time to finally write all of this down.

Finally, we would like to thank our Fern Creek High School family. We know that you have been on this journey with us the entire time, and your professionalism and commitment to our students' learning continue to inspire us every day. We look forward to continuing our work with you as we strive to ensure learning for all.

Solution Tree Press would like to thank the following reviewers:

Courtney Burdick
Apprenticeship Mentor Teacher
Spradling Elementary School
Fort Smith, Arkansas

Molly Capps
Principal
McDeeds Creek Elementary School
Southern Pines, North Carolina

Charlcy Carpenter
Instructional Technology Facilitator
Cleveland County Schools
Lawndale, North Carolina

Amber Gareri
K12 Science Coordinator
Pasadena Independent School District
Pasadena, Texas

Josh Kunnath
Eleventh-Grade English Teacher and Instructional Coach
Highland High School
Bakersfield, California

Elizabeth Love
Principal
Spradling Elementary School
Fort Smith, Arkansas

Katie Madigan
Principal
Taylor Elementary School
Arlington, Virginia

Shanna Martin
Instructional and Technology Coach
Lomira School District
Lomira, Wisconsin

Karen Matteson
Instructional Coach
Cortland Enlarged City School District
Cortland, New York

Jolie Morgan
Instructional Coach and English Instructor
Dallas Center Grimes Schools
Grimes, Iowa

Janel Ross
Principal
Mountain Meadow Elementary School
Buckley, Washington

Katie Saunders
Principal
Anglophone School District West
Woodstock, New Brunswick, Canada

Luke Spielman
Principal
Park View Middle School
Mukwonago, Wisconsin

Elyse Webb
Instructional Coach
South Prairie Elementary School
Grimes, Iowa

Jacqueline E. Yu
Student Services Consultant
Christ the Redeemer Catholic Schools
Calgary, Alberta, Canada

Visit **go.SolutionTree.com/leadership** to download the free reproducibles in this book.

TABLE OF CONTENTS

Reproducibles are in italics.

ABOUT THE AUTHORS

Michelle Marrillia is an instructional coach and educational consultant with nearly three decades of experience in education. Since beginning her career in 1996, she has served as a classroom teacher, school administrator, educational presenter, and professional learning community (PLC) coordinator. She is passionate about training instructional coaches, developing teacher leaders, implementing response to intervention (RTI) systems, and creating practical, sustainable coaching programs.

As part of the leadership team at Fern Creek High School in Louisville, Kentucky, Michelle contributed to the school's transformation from persistently low-achieving in 2010 to proficient in 2015. In 2017, Fern Creek earned Solution Tree's DuFour Award, and in 2016, it received the School Innovation and Change Award from the National Preparedness Leadership Initiative.

Michelle works with schools across the United States. She presents at state and national events to support instructional coaches, teachers, administrators, and district leaders in building high-functioning PLCs. She is also a contributor to *Charting the Course for Leaders: Lessons From Priority Schools in a PLC at Work®*.

Michelle holds a bachelor's degree in biology from Georgetown College, a master's degree in teaching from the University of Louisville, and an administrative certification in instructional leadership from Spalding University.

To learn more about Michelle's work, follow @MichelleMarrill on X or connect with her on LinkedIn (https://linkedin.com/in/michelle-marrillia).

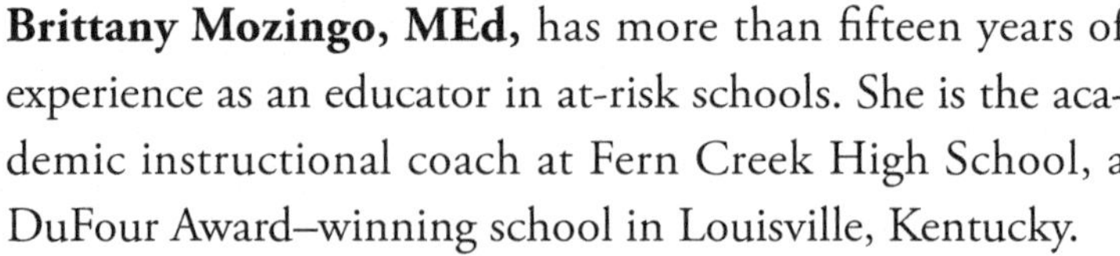

Brittany Mozingo, MEd, has more than fifteen years of experience as an educator in at-risk schools. She is the academic instructional coach at Fern Creek High School, a DuFour Award–winning school in Louisville, Kentucky.

Brittany coaches teacher teams to become accountable members of a highly effective professional learning community. She specializes in cognitive coaching, systems implementation, and assessment literacy.

Brittany earned a bachelor's degree in mathematics and secondary education from Wilmington College and a master's degree in teacher leadership from the University of Louisville. In addition, she has completed thirty postgraduate hours in adult learning theory.

Rebecca Nicolas, EdD, is the principal of Fern Creek High School in Louisville, Kentucky.

Prior to her current role, Rebecca was an assistant principal at Fern Creek and an English teacher and assistant principal at Doss High School, also in Louisville, Kentucky. She has twenty years of experience working in schools with at-risk student populations.

Rebecca's work at Fern Creek involves using data to develop effective teams, implementing the PLC process, and integrating collaborative teams. As one of the few urban turnaround high schools in Kentucky, Fern Creek has received recognition as a Model PLC school. It was a runner-up for the DuFour Award in 2016, and it won the National Preparedness Leadership Initiative's School Innovation and Change Award in 2016 and the DuFour Award in 2017. Rebecca is also a contributor to *Charting the Course for Leaders: Lessons From Priority Schools in a PLC at Work*.

Rebecca earned a bachelor's degree in English from Centre College, a master's degree in English from Wake Forest University, and a doctoral degree in educational leadership from Spalding University.

To book Michelle Marrillia, Brittany Mozingo, or Rebecca Nicolas for professional development, contact pd@SolutionTree.com.

FOREWORD

BY WILLIAM M. FERRITER

The daily life of schools has always carried a sense of urgency. From the first bell, educators juggle everything from instruction and safety to logistics and the priorities of families and communities.

In recent years, though, that urgency has shifted to relentless pressure. More than ever before, principals and coaches face a constant balancing act: covering unstaffed classrooms, fixing broken systems, responding to shifting expectations, and helping students navigate social and emotional struggles that may lie outside the standards we teach but sit at the heart of student success. Against that backdrop, the core purpose of schools—ensuring high levels of learning for every student—can feel dangerously easy to lose sight of. In that environment, only a partnership between the principal and the instructional coach built with clarity and intentionality can move a school forward.

That's why *Together We Lead: How Principals and Instructional Coaches Team Up for Lasting Impact* arrives at just the right moment. The title captures what every school leader and coach has thought at some point: "There just isn't enough time to clarify how we will work with one another." And yet, the central argument of this book is exactly right: Meaningful collaboration between principals and instructional coaches is not a distraction from the work of schools—it is the work that makes everything else possible.

You see, we have plenty of evidence that coaching changes practice and impacts student learning, but coaching can't thrive without systems that protect it. When principals are pulled entirely into managing their buildings, instructional priorities get sidelined. When coaches are used as catchall problem solvers, their core role is diluted. Only when principals and coaches operate interdependently do schools begin to create a culture of coaching—and that is where this book lives.

The credibility of this text comes from the lived experiences of its authors. Michelle, Brittany, and Rebecca are partners who have worked together for more than a decade, designing plans, testing tools, scrapping ideas that didn't work, and continually returning to the central question: How can our partnership move teaching and learning forward no matter how unpredictable the day-to-day experience in our school may be? That experience shows up within this text in practical resources like meeting agendas, priority-setting tools, reflection protocols, and phase-by-phase road maps.

The structure of the book is both simple and powerful. Organized into four phases—(1) setting the stage for collaboration, (2) establishing goals and actions, (3) monitoring and adjusting, and (4) looking ahead—the text offers a logical progression to readers without being rigid. Each phase offers scenarios that will feel authentic to anyone with firsthand experience as a building principal or instructional coach, practical tools for planning and conversation, and reflection protocols to keep one another honest about whether the work is moving forward.

Equally important, the authors resist the temptation to oversimplify. They name the messy realities that every principal and coach has to wrestle with and frame their guidance within that complexity. The message is not "find more hours in the day to collaborate with one another because it matters." The message is "be intentional with the hours you already have so that your collaboration produces results." Clarity of roles, shared goals, and protected time to plan with one another are the non-negotiables that can transform the sometimes-disconnected tasks that principals and coaches tackle each day into focused efforts on behalf of the teachers and students you support.

The book also names a reality that too many principals and coaches have experienced firsthand: the erosion of the coaching role. Coaches pulled into doing cafeteria duty, subbing for classes, or coordinating events may keep the building running in the short term, but the long-term cost of those professional trade-offs is enormous. As the authors argue, this is a false economy. Protecting the integrity of the coaching role is the foundation of both instructional growth and teacher retention.

For all these reasons, *Together We Lead* is both timely and lasting. It speaks to the urgent challenges of today and provides principles and practices that will remain relevant tomorrow. Schools will always be busy. Distractions will always exist. But intentional partnerships between principals and coaches—the kind of instructional leadership that can create the conditions for both adult and student learning to thrive—can always exist, too.

INTRODUCTION

The average morning in any school in the United States could be a study in controlled chaos. Hundreds, or even thousands, of people stream into the school building at the start of the day, each with their own agenda, set of responsibilities, and expectations. And as any educator can attest, the day can go any number of ways. Some days proceed smoothly, moving positively and purposefully toward ensuring the mission and vision of the school. Other days quickly go sideways, as teacher vacancies multiply, class coverage needs to be arranged, parents need to be seen and heard, the building needs to be maintained, and students stray from the path of learning. Every day, educators are pulled from the vital tasks of ensuring learning for all by the siren calls of unanswered emails, cafeteria duty, endless meetings, and the crises that multiply anytime lots of humans are gathered in one space. These distractions may seem innocuous enough in the course of a day, but over time, they can prevent a school leader from focusing on instructional priorities. By creating and maintaining a strong partnership between the principal and the instructional coach, school leaders can ensure they focus on the right work at the right time.

Together We Lead explores the partnership of the principal and instructional coach—a critical element in limiting distractions and ensuring the integrity of a school's instructional priorities. We don't use the word *partnership* lightly; we know that truly impactful, interdependent collaboration between the principal and the coach elevates a school's instructional discourse. When the principal and coach work together, their coaching and collaboration "form the link that connects great leadership, great teaching, and great learning" (Johnson, Leibowitz, & Perret, 2017, p. 11). In the following sections, we will explore how these roles can best be defined and how these two parties must work together to create systems that can withstand the chaos of the average school day.

The Partnership

The principal-coach relationship is one of the most important relationships in the school building. When it is cultivated, it allows both the principal and the coach to fully actualize the potential of their individual roles. In this partnership, the principal's role becomes more firmly rooted in the school's instructional priorities, and the coach's role expands to secure access to the resources and opportunities necessary for doing the job. By creating a powerful partnership, principals and coaches can maximize the influence of their individual roles to become greater than the sum of their parts. Their combined influence can transform both daily decisions about the school's time and focus and long-term goals that require strategic planning and allocation of resources. When a principal and coach work as true partners, they can alter a school community and influence the trajectory of learning for all students.

As far as partnerships are concerned, the authors of this book have worked as partners for over a decade. We have inhabited various roles during that time and supported each other in different incarnations of our careers. After years of working together, we have realized that our work as principal-coach partners is profoundly impactful and that our roles are inextricably intertwined.

We couldn't do this work in isolation, and we don't want to. Over the years, we have created systems and revised systems. We have abandoned "great" ideas that just didn't work and asked hard questions of one another when we didn't follow through on commitments. We continue to push one another to refine our work and ensure that our focus is on student learning. We celebrate each other's strengths and help each other through our challenges.

We know that not all principals and coaches have a long history together and that each team will work differently. We also know that the distractions of a school day change with the seasons and that the work of the principal-coach partnership looks very different from month to month. So in this book, we focus on the systems that sustain our efforts—templates, meeting structures, calendars, and timelines—which can work for any combination of partners committed to the work. Our perspectives are equally represented in the following pages to allow time and space for exploring both roles in the principal-coach partnership.

Role Clarity

While the role of the principal has shifted over the years (Fusarelli & Fusarelli, 2018; Gillis, 2022), the position of principal exists in the consciousness of anyone who has ever been to school. However, the role of instructional coach is relatively new to the education lexicon (Showers & Joyce, 1996). Your school may have someone called an *instructional coach*, but that title may not match the work with which this person is tasked. Conversely, your school may have someone with a different title (that is, resource teacher, assistant principal, or dean) who does all the work this book ascribes to an instructional coach. We have seen educators with many different titles step into the role of instructional coach and do so with integrity by focusing on ensuring instructional priorities. Until our profession universally codifies the term, this role may go by various names, so when we say *instructional coach* in this text, we mean the role that is dedicated to working with teachers and administrators to ensure their professional learning positively impacts student learning.

We don't mean to insinuate that the actual title of a school's instructional coach is not important, because it is. Getting clarity on this may be the first step in building the collaborative partnership between the principal and the coach. Indeed, a school may hire someone to fill a position titled *instructional coach* and proceed to use them in every capacity *but* coaching. One of the primary frustrations of coaches we meet is they are tasked with so many different responsibilities that they don't have time to coach. Coaches may be asked to serve as long-term substitute teachers or building assessment coordinators. Some coaches are asked to organize field trips and PTA meetings, decorate for homecoming dances, and write grant applications. Ironically, some coaches—especially those at schools needing "intensive support"—may spend hours each week simply documenting their school's efforts at improvement, collecting evidence for the frequent audits endemic to schools deemed to be underperforming. (If we seem bitter, it may be because that was our situation in 2010, when we first started to work together.)

In the following pages, we make the case that the principal-coach partnership has the power to transform a school, if for no other reason than each of these roles has the power to remind the other why it exists. Every coach needs the principal to ensure they have the time, space, and resources to do the vital work of ensuring learning for all, and every principal needs the coach to ensure they are focused on what's essential over what's urgent.

Why This Book Is Needed

This writing comes at a critical time in our profession. Since schools reopened after the 2020 COVID-19 shutdown, they have faced unprecedented teacher vacancies and a dearth of qualified teachers. The National Center for Education Statistics (2023) reports, "Eighty-six percent of U.S. K–12 public schools reported challenges hiring teachers for the 2023–24 school year."

Increasingly, it is tempting to assign instructional coaches to classroom rosters when substitute teachers are used long term and teacher postings go unanswered. While we understand the pressure to have coaches step into classrooms as a stop-gap, we fervently believe that this false economy creates more problems than it solves. Schools need the guiding efforts of a strong instructional coach, working in tandem with the principal, to ensure that quality instruction is supported and student learning is prioritized. We fully understand that, as educational leaders Michael Fullan and Jim Knight (2011) state, "the work of coaches is crucial because they change the culture of the school as it relates to instructional [and professional] practice" (p. 52). As principals are increasingly tasked with managing complex logistics, human resources, and safety concerns, the principal-coach relationship keeps student learning the main focus.

What's in This Book

We want to make it clear that this is not explicitly an instructional coaching guide. There are excellent coaching resources, many of which we have used and cite here, but this book focuses on the collaborative work of the principal and instructional coach and envisions the distinct impact this collaboration can have within a school.

This book is for K–12 principals and instructional coaches. It frames the work of the principal-coach partnership in four specific phases. Phase 1 focuses on establishing the foundation for a healthy collaborative relationship. Phase 2 explores goal setting and action planning for partners. Phase 3 guides partners as they monitor their plans and adjust their strategies based on formative data, and phase 4 asks partners to be purposeful in celebrating and looking ahead to their next iteration of their journey through the partnership framework.

Figure I.1 outlines the four phases around which principals and coaches orient their work within the partnership framework.

The partnership framework includes action steps, practical tools, and guiding questions to apply the learning. Each phase of the book includes the following.

- Reflection questions at the beginning and end
- Scenarios that illuminate what challenges the partners may face and how those challenges may play out in varied school environments
- Key moves and essential tools for prioritizing the work, which draw on research and firsthand experiences, as well as recommended strategies for implementing instructional priorities

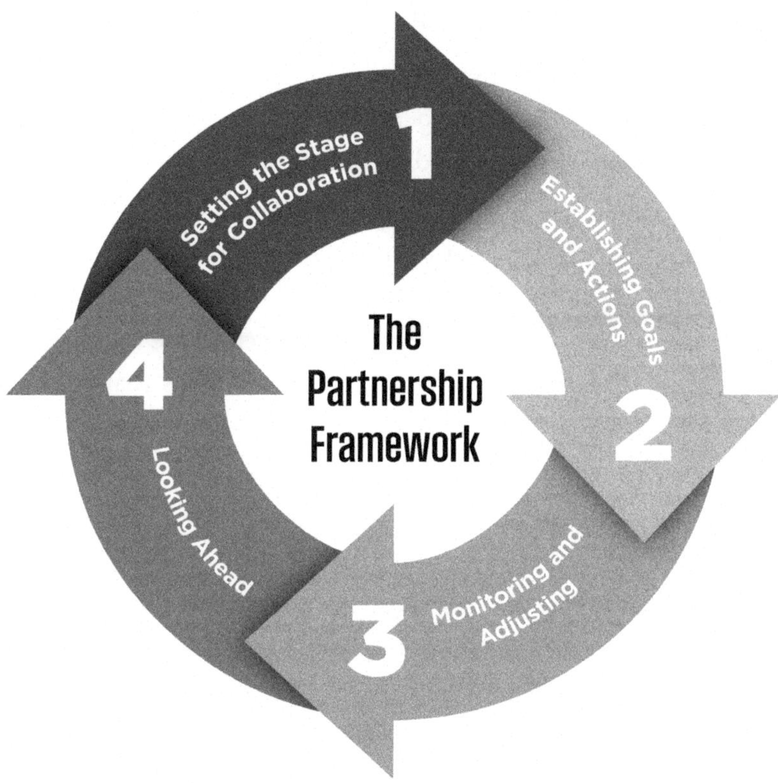

Figure I.1: *The partnership framework.*

- A Calibration Conversations section, in which we explore ways that this work can be derailed or done badly—in many cases, because we learned what *not* to do by doing exactly that
- Principal and instructional coach perspectives that offer insights into the approaches and experiences of both roles, highlight the dynamics of our partnership, and provide strategies that helped us align our efforts
- A read, react, and reflect protocol to help your team explore and avoid the pitfalls that slow the momentum of principal-coach work
- A clear and actionable end-of-chapter checklist for ensuring the principal and coach can assess their progress, identify next steps, and stay focused on what matters most

Phase 1 of the partnership framework entails setting the stage for collaboration. In this phase, partners establish trust, clarify roles and responsibilities, and create clarity regarding the partnership.

Phase 2 includes establishing goals and actions. Here, partners write shared instructional goals, create a partnership plan, and build capacity to empower teacher leaders.

During phase 3, monitoring and adjusting, partners prioritize coaching, measure what matters, and maintain momentum.

Finally, phase 4 involves looking ahead. Partners sustain the work through the analysis of data, celebrate successes and capitalize on wins, and build the foundation for future success through careful planning and allocation of resources.

The appendixes contain detailed supports for partners at every stage of their work. Appendix A (page 105) provides the partnership framework alignment guide, which summarizes the key actions and tools from each phase to help partners calibrate and track progress. Appendix B (page 109) includes yearly, monthly, and weekly calendar templates to help partners plan and sustain collaboration throughout the school year.

Every template and timeline in the following pages is one we have tested, refined, and applied for a variety of teams, teachers, and situations. We know time is the universal limitation of any school leader's attention, so we tracked our efforts using a stopwatch to determine how much time principals and coaches should devote to agenda items, coaching sessions, data collection, and task analysis. As we wrote this book, we dedicated ourselves to learning by doing, and when something didn't work, we committed to letting it go, even when it looked good on paper. We ruthlessly culled the work that didn't speak to the instructional priorities of our school and our collective commitments to one another.

We hope that whatever your title, school, or season of the year, you choose this book to help you make the most of the principal and instructional coach's collaborative efforts. We know that we are extraordinarily lucky to work with people who share our commitment to learning for all and who inspire us to strive together every day. We believe that when the principal and coach work together, their collaborative power can transform each day—even a chaotic one—into a day where they get to do great work. Let's get started!

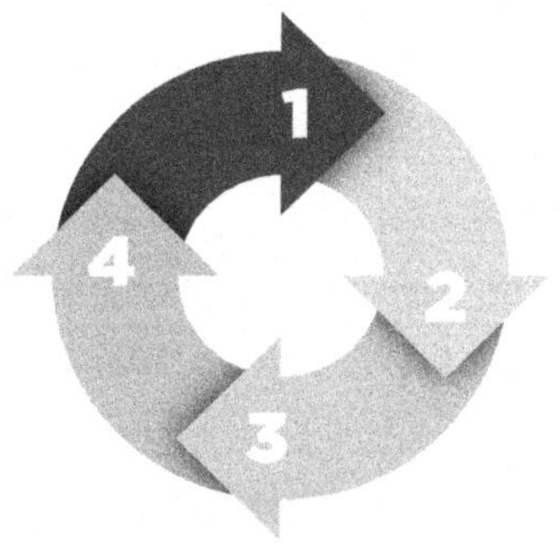

PHASE 1
Setting the Stage for Collaboration

- Establish trust.
- Clarify roles and responsibilities.
- Create clarity regarding the partnership.

Consider the following hypothetical scenario.

When Principal Mendez was hired to lead Midland Middle School, many community members hoped he would clean up the place. He started his tenure by hiring teachers to fill vacancies, beginning long-deferred building maintenance, and establishing systems to ensure smooth transitions between classes. He believed his mandate as principal was to limit disruptions to class time.

Now, three years later, the school feels like it's under control. The hallways are clear and orderly, and teachers are free to teach rather than deal with the distractions of unruly students. However, Principal Mendez is unsure how to shift his focus to supporting teachers instructionally and ensuring professional growth for his staff. His instructional coach has been occupied by coordinating testing, supervising the cafeteria, and helping out in the counseling office. He likes Coach Green, but he doesn't know her very well. They don't meet formally outside of his weekly leadership meetings. He doesn't really know her strengths or interests, but he knows she is a team player and will do whatever the school asks her to do. He recognizes that he needs to meet with her regularly, but even though the school is calmer now, it is very hard to find time in his schedule for meetings. He is sure Coach Green helps teachers when she has the time, but he's not sure what she does or when she does it.

Coach Green has been the instructional coach at Midland Middle School for the last ten years. She loves the kids and respects most of her colleagues, but she recognizes that she constantly has to revise her idea of her job. Principal Mendez is Midland's third principal since she began her tenure here. When he arrived three years ago, she was optimistic that he would prioritize her work and allow her the time and space to truly coach teachers; after all, she had been on the interview committee. He won over all the committee members with his professed commitment to supporting teachers. While he seems energetic and hardworking, the last three years have taught her he is just like his predecessors—he asks her to complete tasks unrelated to her job title. He has little time for or interest in collaborating with her to help teachers succeed. She wonders how long Principal Mendez will be at Midland and hopes the principal after him will finally understand.

Individually, Principal Mendez and Coach Green believe their work is vital. They both value hard work and are committed to their own vision of what a successful school should look like. They both are veteran educators, seasoned enough to know that school is a busy place and that, sometimes, the everyday business of school won't match up with the ideal version of the job they thought they had signed up for, but they keep trying. They continue to show up each day, tackling challenges as they present themselves, occasionally aware that there is a better way for them to work together but unsure of how to get there.

Reflection Questions

Based on the preceding scenario, answer the following questions.

- Think about Principal Mendez and Coach Green's partnership and commitment to supporting student learning. What wins do they achieve as a team? What challenges do they face?
- How would you describe your current partnership with your principal or coach? What have you found to be successful? What hurdles have you encountered while working together?

In any partnership, there inevitably are differences of perspective. Partners may not be on the same page regarding how they should work together; they may disagree about what they must do to meet a shared goal. They may not understand each other's strengths or values; they may not trust each other to do their share. Principal Mendez and Coach Green are competent, well-meaning people who hope that what they do daily is enough to make a difference for students. They don't know how to work together, but the situation is not hopeless. They can set the stage for their collaboration by honoring both their perspectives.

Here, we'll explore the first phase of the partnership framework, where partners create a solid foundation for their partnership. Partners can accomplish this by establishing trust, clarifying the scope of each partner's role and responsibilities, creating norms, and identifying priorities.

Collaboration in Action: Key Moves and Essential Tools

We know powerful partnerships don't happen overnight, but a principal and an instructional coach who are committed to building an interdependent partnership can overcome myriad challenges and capitalize on each other's strengths when they (1) establish trust, (2) clarify roles and responsibilities, and (3) create clarity regarding the partnership. By committing to these action steps in the first phase of the partnership framework, partners build the foundation for their continued work of ensuring learning in their school.

Partners Establish Trust

Interdependence cannot be achieved without trust, but it is obvious that Principal Mendez and Coach Green do not trust each other. They have not had the time and space to develop a trusting relationship, so they continue to work side by side but not together. Their work is not collaborative, and their roles do not intersect. Unfortunately, they will likely continue this way unless they build trust with each other—and this is no easy task. Their situation is challenging, and building trust is never a simple process. These two educators, and even a coach and a principal who have no history at all, have critical work to do to build the trust necessary for collaboration. Professors Roger C. Mayer, James H. Davis, and F. David Schoorman (1995) define *trust* as:

> the willingness of a party to be vulnerable to the actions of another party based on the expectation that the other will perform a particular action important to the trustor, irrespective of the ability to monitor or control that other party. (p. 712)

That vulnerability is difficult when two people are getting to know each other or when patterns of behavior have been established and people's beliefs about one another are entrenched.

Coach Green did not trust the school's two previous principals and is increasingly disillusioned with the current one. Principal Mendez has a nagging feeling that he could better capitalize on Coach Green's expertise and feels guilty for asking her to take on extraneous duties unrelated to her job title. A coach and a principal with no history together may be reluctant to engage with an unknown entity; however, to get what they need from each other, these parties may need to focus on understanding the other party's needs instead of their own.

In *Harvard Business Review*, Frances X. Frei and Anne Morriss (2020) urge leaders who are trying to build trust to start with empathy and "work to ensure that everyone else gets what they need." For a partnership to flourish, one must employ empathy and dial into what the other person requires. In fact, one of the first exercises we recommend for partners is that they have a frank conversation about what they need from the other person. This vulnerability engenders greater trust and the beginning of an authentic partnership. Activities in this phase are meant to facilitate partner interactions, to build understanding of each other's working styles, and to create the conditions for collaboration.

The psychology of building trust at work is a field with a significant amount of research, and one that continues to evolve as organizations evolve. Researchers Kurt T. Dirks and Bart de Jong (2022) find that understanding the way trust is gained and maintained has the power "to make organizations and teams function more smoothly, to make workplaces more humane, and to promote collaborative work to address important organizational challenges" (p. 269). Partners can establish the interdependence of a healthy principal-coach partnership only when they trust each other. The effort they put into building trust will pay dividends for their continued success.

Consider these actions for building trust in your partnership.

- Be reliable by delivering on shared commitments and meeting deadlines.
- Be transparent by speaking openly and honestly about challenges.
- Be consistent by setting clear expectations and following through with commitments.
- Communicate clearly by actively listening and promptly responding.
- Show respect by honoring confidentiality and expressing appreciation.
- Stay flexible by embracing change and focusing on solutions.

Principals Supporting Coaches

In addition to exhibiting vulnerability and empathy, a principal can create trust with a coach by communicating their values. Principal Mendez, like all principals, conveys his values to the school community through implicit and explicit communication, the creation of the daily schedule, and the allocation of resources. A principal who seeks to support the school's coach makes the time to meet with them, speaks to other staff about the importance of the coach's work, and creates the conditions for that work to have an impact. The first move for Principal Mendez will be to protect Coach Green's time. There will be times when it's appropriate to have all hands on deck for an urgent task, but an instructional coach should spend most of their day providing support and feedback to teachers to help them improve their practices.

Education experts Jacy Ippolito and Rita M. Bean (2019) state, "Principals can more effectively build a culture of coaching by working with coaches to create schedules that allow them to engage in one-on-one, small-group, and large-group coaching activities and address both individual and system needs." When principals structure time for these varied coaching interactions, it signals to the staff that coaching is a priority in the school. Unfortunately, coaches often report that they are assigned duties that don't align with their vision of the role.

Research shows that principals who describe coaching as valuable positively influence the time coaches spend observing and providing feedback to teachers (Matsumura, Sartoris, Bickel, & Garnier, 2009). A principal who wishes to support their coach must do so in word and deed. In their book *Coaching Matters*, Joellen Killion, Cindy Harrison, Chris Bryan, and Heather Clifton (2012) suggest, "As the chief advocate for coaching, a principal's behaviors toward the coach and their communication about the importance of coaching and continuous improvement have a significant influence on the overall success of the coaching initiative" (p. 100). By protecting his coach's time, Principal Mendez will affirm his commitment to helping teachers improve their practice. School community members will recognize that he prioritizes their learning needs by protecting the coaching role and maintaining the integrity of a coaching culture.

Coaches Supporting Principals

Coach Green doesn't trust Principal Mendez to value her work, but the reality is that she has not advocated for what she needs from him to do her job effectively. She has taken on tasks that are not really part of a coach's job because she wants to be perceived as a team player, but she resents spending time on them. She has not asked Principal Mendez for his time because she thinks he will put her off or turn her away. Instead, she avoids him and nurses her suspicions that he wouldn't want to engage in a real coaching conversation.

Coaches should be empowered to coach while supporting the principal by recognizing that they are part of a larger school team. Instructional coaching must occur within the larger school culture and work with other systems, not against them or in isolation. While coaching is critical, a coach should also be willing to pitch in with other duties when needed. School-day supervision duties, for example, are necessary to maintain safe and orderly school operations. If the leadership team is responsible for these duties, the coach should participate too. In our partnership, some of our best collaborative epiphanies happen while we're supervising the cafeteria. Our culture values a collective lift for some of our less desirable activities, and a coach can build relationships and credibility by pitching in when needed. The key is to strike a balance. Coaches should understand that occasional shared duties will strengthen trust, but such duties should not overshadow the core purpose of the coaching role. Coaches can strike this balance by communicating clearly with the principal.

The Partnership Perspective

PRINCIPAL & COACH INSIGHTS

PRINCIPAL PERSPECTIVE: *Rebecca*

When I first became a principal, I felt people needed to see me being busy. This was how they would know I was working hard for them. I prided myself on getting more than ten thousand steps a day, and when I was too tired to exercise after work, I comforted myself with the thought, *Administration is my cardio.* When my instructional coach would pop her head into my office and ask, "Do you have a quick minute?," more often than not, I didn't. I was so busy doing a million things. Looking back, though, I can't remember what any of them were. Many of them felt like urgent tasks, but they had little to no relation to ensuring the mission and vision of our school. I had endless checklists that I was constantly checking, but I did not structure my day to allow time for collaborative work with the professionals in my building who would best inform our continuous improvement efforts. I believed that coaching was important, but it existed for me in the abstract. My beliefs didn't align with my actions, as I wasn't making the time or space to create a meaningful partnership with my coach.

COACH PERSPECTIVE: *Michelle*

When I first began my career as a coach, I tried to find my place in the school. No longer a teacher yet not quite an administrator, I understood that my role was to support the school's instructional efforts. I also believed in assisting with immediate tasks or issues as they arose. If I could alleviate some of the burdens on the principal, the school's overall functioning would improve, resulting in better teaching and enhanced student learning. My principal at the time advised me to focus on two essential areas—(1) instruction and (2) everything that supports it—a charge that meant learning when to step back as much as when to step in. That guidance has stayed with me and reminds me that I do not need to attend every meeting or be in the middle of every conversation. Sometimes, I have to check my ego, trusting that my absence will allow me to stay focused on our instructional mission. Conversely, I can provide gentle reminders when we need to recalibrate and realign our instructional priorities. This delicate balance taught me that effective coaching is not about taking on every task but about prioritizing what matters most for teaching and learning.

Partners Establish Norms

In a busy work environment, the time it takes to focus on what your partner needs from you seems like a luxury, but this actually is a critical investment in establishing the bedrock of trust needed to drive change. Both parties should commit to meeting regularly with fidelity, and they should do it face-to-face. In their review of the literature on the development of trust at work, Dirks and de Jong (2022) find that "face-to-face communication facilitates trust, compared to other modes of communication" (p. 259). Simply sitting at a table with someone doesn't ensure they will come to trust you, but when you can block off time, put away devices, look them in the eye, and be vulnerable, you are demonstrating that you value your partner's time and expertise. You will engender trust by establishing norms that guide how you and your partner interact over time and ultimately learn together.

Establishing norms is foundational to the principal-coach framework. Norms serve as the pathway to developing trust and mutual respect between the principal and the coach and ensuring their ability to contribute to shared school-improvement goals. Researchers Christine Horne and Stefanie Mollborn (2020) suggest that norms promote social order, which, in this context, encourages cooperation to support collective outcomes. Explicit norms create a space for productive communication, reflective dialogue, and risk taking. The authors of *Learning by Doing* (DuFour et al., 2024) further emphasize that teams perform at higher levels when expectations for procedures, responsibilities, and relationships are clearly defined.

Norms for Existing Partnerships

This book details, in part, the journey we have taken to create our own principal-coach partnership. It is the product of fifteen years of working together in various roles, not just principal and coach. We have also been teachers and assistant principals in various iterations of our school during audits, crises, and one very disruptive pandemic. What has emerged is not a static understanding of our roles or what we need from one another; these things continue to evolve. We have learned to listen better and look harder at what makes a difference for teachers and students. We continue to revisit the topic of norms to ensure that we value what matters to our partners and move toward our goals while honoring our counterparts' learning and working styles in this process. Establishing norms for working together is vital, even if you and your partner have worked together for years. Indeed, it may be even more important for colleagues who are very familiar with one another, as they are most likely to make assumptions about what the other needs.

If you have an existing partnership, we urge you to make establishing and revisiting norms a priority. Schedule time to discuss expectations, communication styles, and what support looks like for each of you. The sample tool for establishing norms introduced in figure 1.1 is just as valuable for veteran partners as it is for new ones. Dedicating time to this process strengthens collaboration, boosts productivity, and helps you adapt as roles and priorities evolve. Norms are the guardrails that help new and long-standing partners avoid misunderstandings and leverage the full strength of their partnership.

While Principal Mendez and Coach Green have worked in the same building for three years, they do not have an existing partnership. For this pair, an honest conversation that establishes norms could potentially mitigate some of the distrust or guilt they are carrying about their interactions with each other. It could help them see a new way of being and moving forward concerning their respective roles. Their challenge may not be the same as one faced by a newly hired principal or coach, but figure 1.1 will be equally impactful for them if they take it in good faith and honor the resulting norms in each of their principal-coach interactions.

Norms for New Partnerships

If you are forming a new partnership, we suggest that establishing norms be one of your first priorities. Have an initial meeting to learn about each individual's

Before-Meeting Action	Spend ten minutes reflecting on the following prompts.
During-Meeting Actions	Each partner will have two minutes to share their reflections with the team. After each partner has shared, create a list of three to five norms.
When I am listening, I need . . . *to ensure my device is away. Sometimes, taking notes on sticky notes helps me listen, and then I use the notes to paraphrase what I heard. (I am always looking for ways to practice my coaching skills!)*	
When I am looking at data, I need . . . *time to explore at first (either before or after the meeting), but then we should have a protocol to help us focus on our priorities. I think it's important to answer the question, "What are we looking for in the data?"*	
When I am planning, I need . . . *time to think! I don't like to be surprised and have to plan on the spot. If we're planning, I need time to think prior to meeting, or else be prepared for a mean-looking thinking face.*	
When I am reflecting, I need . . . *to reflect out loud. I am constantly reflecting, so talking it out sometimes helps me process my reflections.*	
I will consider the meeting successful when . . . *we are productive and accomplish what we say we will.*	
I will consider the meeting unsuccessful when . . . *we go rogue and accomplish nothing, and the norms aren't followed.*	
One norm I would like us to adhere to is . . . *the agenda for the next meeting will be set at the end of every meeting.*	
Our Norms: • *We will allow processing time as needed ("Hold up, I need a minute").* • *We will create a meeting agenda and send a reminder twenty-four hours prior to the meeting.* • *We will put phones away during the meeting.*	

Figure 1.1: *Sample discussion tool for establishing norms.*
Visit ***go.SolutionTree.com/leadership*** *for a free reproducible version of this figure.*

communication, planning, and thinking styles. Figure 1.1 provides prompts to guide your conversation and will help you and your partner build trust, create clarity, and set the tone for how the two of you will work together.

Before your initial meeting, take some time to reflect on your needs and how you might communicate them in the meeting. This will help you identify what your partner should know about how you prefer to listen, observe, plan, reflect, and meet. Figure 1.1 (page 15) includes reflection prompts you can complete beforehand to prepare for the discussion and facilitate the meeting; it shows how a participant might work with the tool.

During your initial meeting, discuss your responses to figure 1.1. What essential listening traits of yours does your principal or coach need to know about? Are you a notetaker? When thinking through a new idea, do you need extra processing time? Do you prefer to reflect silently or process aloud? What are you hoping to get out of your scheduled meeting time? We recommend spending ten to fifteen minutes listening to and learning more about your teammate, whether you have worked with your teammate for years or are just beginning the partnership. Taking the time to learn more about how each person works will help establish trust and strengthen collaboration.

Following the discussion, you and your partner should create a list of three to five norms to clarify expectations and guide your work together. You can record these notes in your copy of the discussion tool.

Partners Clarify Roles and Responsibilities

We refer to the principal-coach *partnership* throughout this text and use that terminology intentionally. As partners, a principal and a coach are both responsible for ensuring that the school prioritizes instructional goals, even while they occupy very different roles in the process. Each role has its own access and influence and carries a distinct set of responsibilities. Understanding the interdependence of those roles allows both the principal and the coach to leverage their positions for maximum impact. Killion and colleagues (2012) find that "when their working relationship begins, astute coaches and principals create a formal partnership agreement that describes how they will work together to carry out their shared passion for their school" (p. 101).

Coaching expert Lucy West (2017) explores the interaction of principal and coach as partners and posits that role clarity can contribute to a positive coaching culture. She argues that when educators at every level—teachers, coaches, and principals—work collaboratively across roles, they enhance the overall capacity of the school system. This interdependence is critical to the success of any partnership and requires frank conversations about who is doing what and why they are doing it. You can't have an effective baseball team if everyone only knows how to play second base. Each player must know their role, as well as the roles of the other players on the field, to leverage their strengths and play strategically.

Taking inventory of the tasks required for each role is a quick way to see where you and your partner spend time. You and your partner should conduct these audits early in your work together to establish role clarity, and then again throughout the phases of your partnership to check your fidelity to those roles during different seasons of the school year. Figure 1.2 shows how principals and coaches can clarify the essential tasks for creating a meaningful and doable coaching schedule.

Directions: This tool helps with determining the instructional coach's roles and responsibilities. To begin this process, the coach and principal should compile a comprehensive list of the instructional coach's daily, weekly, and monthly tasks. This list should also include less frequent tasks such as open houses and testing. After completing the task list, answer the reflection questions.

Daily Tasks	Weekly Tasks	Monthly Tasks	Occasional Tasks
Supervise cafeteria duty. *Respond to teacher coaching requests.* *Review teacher lesson plans for feedback.* *Monitor progress on coaching cycles.*	*Attend team meetings.* *Coach teachers.* *Attend the leadership team meeting.* *Complete teacher walkthroughs.* *Check in with team leads.* *Co-plan with teachers.* *Model lessons or co-teach.* *Debrief after classroom visits.* *Analyze team and student data.* *Cover classes.* *Write lesson plans for absent teachers.*	*Attend the faculty meeting.* *Attend the department meeting.* *Attend the instructional leadership team meeting.* *Meet with the literacy team.* *Meet with the equity team.* *Attend district level coaching meetings.* *Review SMART goals with the team leaders.* *Organize principal-coach walkthroughs.* *Enter data for school and district initiatives.*	*Attend open house.* *Facilitate staff professional development days.* *Assist with state testing or proctoring.* *Help coordinate instructional rounds.* *Organize schoolwide events (that is, district or state visits, parent-teacher conferences, teacher appreciation week, and staff celebrations).*

Review the tasks and consider how each supports your school's mission and vision. Are there any tasks that you need to remove?

Not all these tasks require equal focus from me at all times. There are several valuable culture-building tasks that I may not need to prioritize over high-impact coaching work. Tasks to be considered for reprioritization include:

- *Covering classes*
- *Organizing staff celebrations*

Figure 1.2: *Sample identifying roles and responsibilities tool.*

continued →

- *Completing noninstructional data tasks*
- *Participating in committee work*

Consider your edited list and your school's mission and vision, and note any tasks that you need to add.

To stay aligned with our mission and vision, I must prioritize tasks that directly impact teaching and learning. Task to be considered as top priorities include:

- *Completing coaching cycles*
- *Supporting collaborative teams and the professional learning community*
- *Completing instructional learning walks and providing feedback to teachers*

Reflection:

1. Based on the identified tasks, is the proposed schedule for the instructional coach realistic and manageable?

   Based on our initial review of the current coaching schedule, the principal and I need to revise timelines to better meet the school's needs. After reviewing the priorities, we will collaborate to make a doable schedule that addresses our identified priorities.
2. How will we communicate the instructional coach's schedule to the faculty and staff to ensure transparency and understanding?

   We will share the weekly schedule in the shared digital calendar and post it in the shared staff workspace.
3. What methods will the coach and principal use to regularly assess the effectiveness and impact of the instructional coach's schedule?

   We will review the coaching calendar at the principal-coach meetings to reflect on progress and make adjustments as needed.

Visit ***go.SolutionTree.com/leadership*** *for a free reproducible version of this figure.*

Jim Knight, founder of the Instructional Coaching Group, has explored the coaching role; his research has been instrumental to our understanding of the unique space that coaches occupy in a school. Knight (2022) posits that when a coach is empowered to do the right work, they "(1) establish a clear picture of reality; (2) set emotionally compelling, student-focused goals; and (3) learn, adapt, and integrate teaching practices that help teachers and students hit goals" (p. x). He says, "That kind of comprehensive learning is next to impossible for busy educators to achieve without a coach" (Knight, 2022, p. x).

The value of an instructional coach is amplified when they can act as a liaison between the leadership team and the teaching staff. They inhabit a space that allows them to provide feedback untethered from required supervision protocols and to tailor professional learning to the entire faculty or an individual teacher. When they create a powerful partnership with the principal, they also have the capacity to influence the time and money that is allocated to instructional priorities, and, in the best-case scenarios, can help steer the ship back to those priorities when new initiatives and tempting distractions arise.

It's important to note that there is a difference between understanding and valuing the benefits of coaching and actually being a coach. Supervisors can adopt a coaching mindset when giving feedback, but that doesn't make them coaches, nor should it. A school needs a principal *and* a coach working together to ensure both can do their jobs.

The coach's role is to support long-term development, while the principal's role is to ensure that schoolwide goals are met. Over time, instructional coaches develop a skill set grounded in adult learning theory, reflective practices, and structured feedback loops. They practice and refine these skills to support teachers in developing their craft. The principal and coach roles are complementary—not a one-or-the-other proposition. The principal guides the school in its mission and vision, while the coach supports the school's professional development and instructional growth.

We caution school leadership teams against role confusion. They may often refer to their school administrators as *instructional leaders*, which some minds may translate as *instructional coaches*. When those terms become conflated, teachers may receive mixed messages, and the focus of coaching may shift from intentional, strategic instructional coaching to surface-level feedback. While principals and supervisors can provide feedback through a coaching lens, it is critical to have a coach to ensure consistent, purposeful guidance. A designated coach gives teachers a safe space to reflect and grow outside the evaluation cycle. Figure 1.3 (page 20) features a tool that principals and coaches can use to define the unique roles and responsibilities of each position and ensure that instructional leadership and coaching remain aligned and focused on supporting teacher growth.

Partners Create Clarity Regarding the Partnership

The next step for principals and coaches in setting the stage for collaboration is to get crystal clear on the parameters of the partnership. This includes determining work logistics: the time you will allocate for tasks and the systems you will use to track your progress toward goals. Like most educators, we love a good template and have included examples of the templates that guide our work and keep us organized. Partners must have frank conversations about what tools they will use, which platforms they will rely on to store data, and how they will communicate with one another (via email, shared documents, and so on). Clarity precedes competence (Schmoker, 2004), and the time spent on creating a clear vision of how and where

Directions: This tool helps with determining the differences between the instructional coach's and the principal's instructional leadership responsibilities. To begin this process, respond to the following reflection questions.

- What are the principal's instructional responsibilities?
    - *Establish clear schoolwide goals.*
    - *Promote high-quality instruction.*
    - *Ensure curriculum is standards aligned and meets the needs of students.*
    - *Monitor instruction and student engagement by regularly visiting classrooms.*
    - *Encourage teacher collaboration.*
    - *Provide meaningful feedback and coaching to teachers.*
    - *Analyze student performance data.*
    - *Communicate with families and staff.*
    - *Ensure teachers have access to resources needed to implement high-quality instruction.*
    - *Create schedules that maximize instructional time and provide time for teacher collaboration.*
- What are the coach's instructional responsibilities?
    - *Collaborate with individual teachers, teacher teams, and the leadership team.*
    - *Provide coaching and feedback to individual teachers and teacher teams.*
    - *Provide instructional support through modeling, co-teaching, and classroom observations.*
    - *Design and facilitate targeted professional development that is aligned with school goals and tied to best practices.*
    - *Support individual and team goal setting.*
    - *Analyze student performance data with teachers to inform instruction.*

Next, complete the following Venn diagram. Where are there opportunities for collaboration between the instructional coach and the principal?

- *Analyzing student performance data*
- *Establishing goals*
- *Providing feedback and coaching*

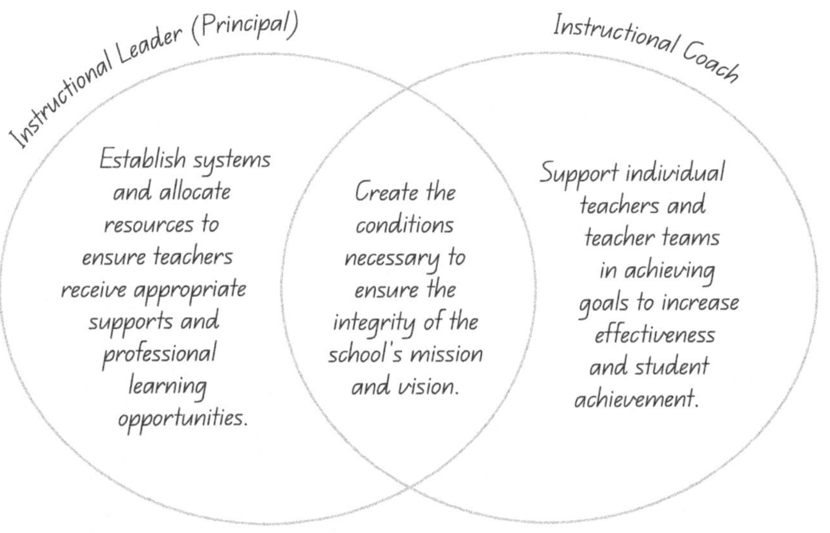

Figure 1.3: *Example discussion tool for instructional leadership roles.*

Visit ***go.SolutionTree.com/leadership*** *for a free reproducible version of this figure.*

the work will proceed is an investment in the partnership that will help avoid conflict and confusion moving forward.

Of course, clarity is not just a big-picture idea; it has to show up in the daily routines of the partnership. The following subsections highlight how partners communicate, schedule and protect time for collaboration, and organize their work. By being intentional in each of these areas, principals and coaches create the conditions for a partnership that is efficient and sustainable.

Communication and Collaboration

All effective collaboration starts with clear and consistent communication. Figure 1.4 shows a calendar template you can use with your partner to ensure that you prioritize collaboration. For more calendars, see the reproducibles, "Year at a Glance," "Monthly Calendar," and "Weekly Planning and Reflection" in appendix B (page 109). We recommend that principals and coaches meet at least two times per month. However, it can be hard to schedule time to meet during certain months or times of year. Decide on the best time to meet by looking at your school calendar and weekly schedule. Will you meet once a week at a specific time and location? Will dates and times need to be flexible due to other scheduled meetings or school events? Once you confirm meeting dates, put them on the calendar and protect that scheduled collaboration time. Should there be a week when you need to reschedule a meeting, ensure that you and your partner reschedule it within seven days, or else there is a good chance the meeting won't happen.

We commit to meeting on the following dates. (Aim for two meetings per month.)
If a meeting needs to be canceled, we will reschedule it within seven days.

Month	Date	Location	Time	**Key Topics to Consider for This Meeting** (For example, a summer faculty retreat, schoolwide testing, or student conferences)
June				
June				
July				
July				
August				
August				
September				

Figure 1.4: *Meeting planner template.*

Visit ***go.SolutionTree.com/leadership*** *for a free reproducible version of this figure.*

Priorities

During this initial phase of collaboration, the principal and coach must identify the coaching priorities they will focus on during the school year. While collaboration is a useful tool, it is effective only when tied to meaningful and focused work. Richard DuFour and colleagues (2024) assert, "Collaboration does not lead to improved results unless people are focused on the right work. Collaboration is a means to an end, not the end itself" (p. 19). After identifying priorities, you each must take time to individually reflect on how a coaching culture supports your school's mission and vision and will ensure progress on school goals. Use figures 1.5 and 1.6 to begin creating a vision for what a coaching culture looks like at your school.

Before-Meeting Actions:

- Identify key coaching priorities aligned to your school's mission and goals.
- Spend ten minutes reflecting on the following questions.
- Record each response on a sticky note, and bring the responses to the meeting.

Reflection Questions:

- How would a coaching culture support the school's mission and ensure we meet our school goals?
- What would a coaching culture at our school look like by the end of the school year?

Figure 1.5: *Tool for setting priorities—Individual reflection.*

*Visit **go.SolutionTree.com/leadership** for a free reproducible version of this figure.*

During-Meeting Actions:

- Share sticky note reflections.
- Sort the sticky notes into groups based on their connections to the school's mission.
- Create a "coaching priority" label for each group.
- Discuss the following reflection questions for each coaching priority.

Reflection Questions:

- Does this coaching priority directly support our school's mission? Will it ensure that we meet our school goals?
- What level of implementation would we rate this coaching priority—not in place, partially in place, or fully in place? What evidence do we have to support this rating?

- Does this coaching priority have a direct impact on student learning? If yes, how does it compare to the other priorities?
- Is this coaching priority equitable? Will it impact all teachers? All students?
- Is this a coaching priority our team wants to focus on this school year?

Coaching Priorities:

As a team, we will focus on the following coaching priorities this school year.

Figure 1.6: *Tool for setting priorities—Collaborative discussion.*
Visit ***go.SolutionTree.com/leadership*** *for a free reproducible version of this figure.*

Partners Hold Each Other Accountable

Once your team has agreed on when to meet and what to focus on, you must decide how to structure the meeting time. When planning for the meeting, you will want to agree on three to five actions you will collaborate on during the scheduled time. These actions should revolve around the school's instructional and coaching priorities and align with the mission and vision.

Figure 1.7 shows how a team might use a template to create an agenda for the principal-coach meeting. Agendas will hold your team accountable for completing the work on time and help you monitor the outcomes of your meetings. To be as efficient as possible, you and your partner will complete some agreed-on actions before your meetings. You should make these agreements as you set the agenda at the end of the previous meeting. Also, committing to listening, looking at data, planning, and reflecting during every meeting are important. These four actions reinforce strong coaching practices and ensure that time is spent productively.

Meeting Date: *August 29*

Before-Meeting Actions:

☑ *Send the agenda the day prior to the meeting.*
☑ *Complete a learning walk one-pager.*
☑ *Use the professional development period tracker.*

Our Norms:

- *We will allow processing time ("Hold up, I need a minute").*
- *We will create a meeting agenda and send a reminder twenty-four hours prior to the meeting.*
- *We will put phones away during the meeting.*

Figure 1.7: *Sample meeting agenda.*

continued →

Action:	**Products:**	**Next Steps:**
Action: *Facilitator training updates (5 minutes)*	**Products:** *Current school year action steps*	**Next Steps:** *Finalize the facilitator training plan.*
Action: *Learning walk protocol (5 minutes)*	**Products:** • *Learning walk tracker* • *Learning walk planning conversations* • *Learning walk reflection conversation* • *Learning walk one-pager*	**Next Steps:** *Schedule the coach's first round of learning walks with the administrators.*
Action: *Professional development period tracker analysis (10 minutes)*	**Products:** *Professional development period tracker*	**Next Steps:** *Follow-ups include:* • *Geometry—Pacing calendar* • *Civics—Shared agenda* • *English I—Curriculum supports*
Action: *Admin and coach meeting agenda (25 minutes)*	**Products:** *Professional development period tracker*	**Next Steps:** *Send calendar invites for upcoming principal, assistant principal, and coach meetings.*
Next Meeting Date: *September 26* **Location and Time:** *Main office, third period* **What to Do Before the Next Meeting:** *Update action step reflections.*		

Visit ***go.SolutionTree.com/leadership*** *for a free reproducible version of this figure.*

Calibration Conversations

Even partners who have actively set the stage for collaboration must occasionally revisit their commitments to calibrate their experiences with the process and with one another. At the end of each phase, we invite partners to consider scenarios that explore how they might sometimes lose their way. Read each scenario and imagine it playing out in your own context. How would you react if this were your partnership? Use the read, react, and reflect protocol in figure 1.8 to compare your own practices to those in the scenarios, and identify ways to strengthen your work together.

Protocol	1. Determine the partnership's progress for each scenario as it relates to: • Establishing trust • Clarifying roles and responsibilities • Creating clarity regarding the partnership 2. Discuss the potential next step for this partnership.
Scenario 1	Coach Green looks forward to her weekly coaching meeting with the principal. She has ideas for how she can help teams set SMART goals and track their progress toward student mastery of essential standards. Her meeting with Principal Mendez is set for after school on Thursday, so she waits in his office to get started. One of their norms is communicating quickly and clearly if something keeps them from meeting. Soon, a text from Principal Mendez arrives, saying that there was a fight among students as they were boarding the bus and he won't be able to make the meeting. He asks when they can reschedule, but Coach Green is so disappointed that she packs up and leaves school without responding. She knew he wasn't really invested in this process, and this just proves it.
Scenario 2	Principal Mendez and Coach Green have added time for them to meet to their calendars, and they protect that time. Coach Green is waiting outside Principal Mendez's office door for Thursday's meeting as he finishes meeting with the school's assistant principal and counselor. As these administrators exit the office, Coach Green can hear them discussing the district-required learning walk protocols the principal just presented. She thinks learning walks fall within her purview and doesn't know why she wasn't included in the conversation.
Scenario 3	After working through new partnership protocols with Coach Green for several months, Principal Mendez is a convert. He is so excited about the impact that coaching can have on the school's instructional culture that he declares the next order of business is to make all the administrators and teacher leaders into coaches. While Coach Green appreciates his new enthusiasm, she is worried. She knows that when everyone is a coach, no one is a coach. She doesn't want to put a damper on their burgeoning partnership, but she knows she has to say something to ensure the clarity and consistency of their roles.

Figure 1.8: *Read, react, and reflect protocol.*

Final Thoughts

As partners, we sometimes discuss which classrooms we should visit with the teachers we are trying to coach. Generally, we find that having a struggling teacher observe a master teacher is not always the best choice. A master teacher is usually so adept at their craft that all the teaching moves look effortless. It is not easy to perceive the decisions they're making, the strategies they're employing, or the strings they're pulling. It is usually more fruitful to visit a teacher who is working to improve and who employs specific strategies that we can *see* when we are in the room.

We believe the same holds true for powerful partnerships, which is why they can be difficult to replicate. To the naked eye, a partnership may seem effortless; the two parties appear to be magically in sync as they finish each other's sentences and anticipate each other's needs. A casual observer may think the partners lucked out, getting to work with someone for whom they have a natural affinity. In reality, many interactions led to that ease and familiarity.

The work of the first phase creates the conditions so those interactions can have the maximum impact for your school. The activities we have described in this chapter all come directly from our own meetings, and we have refined them to set the stage for your collaboration to proceed as efficiently and effectively as possible. Even though we have worked together for a long time, we go back to these processes time and again to ensure that our foundation is strong and that we value our partners as professionals. The principal and coach who commit to setting the stage for collaboration are well on their way to creating an interdependent partnership that will empower them for the next phase: setting goals and taking action to drive their work.

When working with your partner, consider the actions listed in figure 1.9. Complete each action in the checklist to ensure you fully implement phase 1.

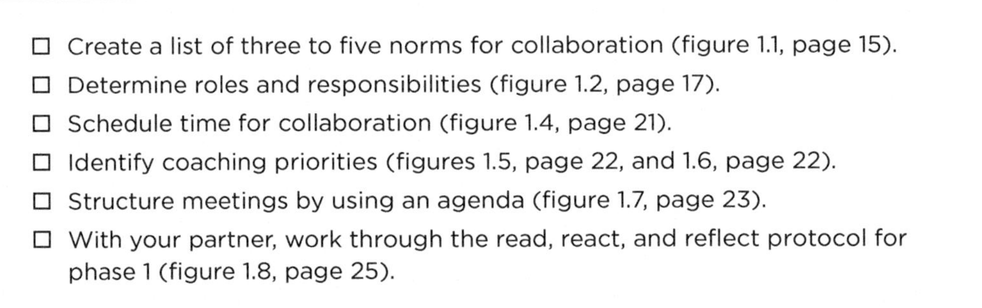

- ☐ Create a list of three to five norms for collaboration (figure 1.1, page 15).
- ☐ Determine roles and responsibilities (figure 1.2, page 17).
- ☐ Schedule time for collaboration (figure 1.4, page 21).
- ☐ Identify coaching priorities (figures 1.5, page 22, and 1.6, page 22).
- ☐ Structure meetings by using an agenda (figure 1.7, page 23).
- ☐ With your partner, work through the read, react, and reflect protocol for phase 1 (figure 1.8, page 25).

Figure 1.9: *Phase 1 checklist—Setting the stage for collaboration.*
Visit ***go.SolutionTree.com/leadership*** *for a free reproducible version of this figure.*

Pause to Reflect II

Reflect on the following questions as you close out phase 1.

- What structures do you currently have to establish trust, clarify roles and responsibilities, and create clarity regarding your partnership?
- What tools does your team need to start using to support collaboration?

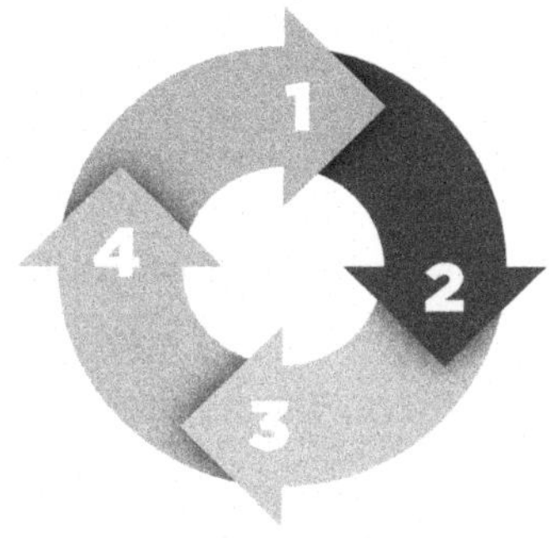

PHASE 2

Establishing Goals and Actions

- Write shared instructional goals.
- Create a partnership plan.
- Build capacity to empower teacher leaders.

Consider the following hypothetical scenario.

Coach Brown is a new instructional coach at Tillson High School, and he is excited to get started. He will miss interacting with students every day as a classroom teacher; however, he knows he can work with teachers to ensure they are learning and growing in their professional practice.

Coach Brown's first days at his new school are a whirlwind. The principal is welcoming, but she also seems to expect that he will tackle all the school's instructional priorities in his first few weeks. He thought he would have time to get to know the teachers and to find his niche in the school culture, but at his first sit-down with the principal, he walks away with a list that includes (1) writing a professional learning plan, (2) revising the literacy plan, (3) meeting with each team leader, (4) attending all team meetings, (5) creating the school-improvement plan, and (6) leading a faculty session on assessment literacy. He knows the principal values his role, but she seems to think he is superhuman and, apparently, the only one responsible for ensuring quality instruction happens in the school. He misses his classroom and wishes he had given this "promotion" more thought.

Principal Jones is so grateful to have Coach Brown at Tillson. She has been juggling dozens of different priorities and is relieved to off-load some of them now that she has a new instructional coach. Coach Brown seemed a little overwhelmed during their first sit-down, but Principal Jones hopes he will quickly jump into the fray. She is exhausted from managing all the moving parts of the school. Her inbox is overflowing with competing demands and special interests representing the district's various departments. She knows she needs to focus, but each ping of her email leads her in a new direction, and she jumps from activity to activity without a plan that aligns her efforts with her school's mission and vision.

Reflection Questions

Based on the preceding scenario, answer the following questions.

- Consider Coach Brown and Principal Jones's first interaction. What goals do they share?
- If you were Principal Jones, how might you adjust the agenda for the first meeting with Coach Brown?
- How would you describe your current interactions with your partner? What things do you discuss? How do you know if you are moving toward your goals?

Coach Brown and Principal Jones have a common interest: Both want teachers to engage in meaningful professional learning that improves student achievement. However, they are overwhelmed by the sheer number of tasks within their job descriptions. Instead of working together to plan their efforts, they will work alongside each other, each ticking off boxes and trying to resolve issues as they manifest. Unfortunately, Tillson High School does not have a culture of collaboration, so unless something changes, these two will forge ahead in their own lanes, not in alignment with each other's efforts. They need to build their capacity as interdependent partners, but not even the most aligned partners can do this work alone. For these partners to meet their goals, they must also build capacity with team and teacher leaders and guarantee that the formidable task of ensuring student learning is a collective commitment for all.

Here, we'll explore phase 2 of the partnership framework, where partners establish goals and action steps. Partners can accomplish this by writing SMART goals, creating a partnership plan, fostering ongoing reflection, celebrating progress, and building capacity.

Collaboration in Action: Key Moves and Essential Tools

Creating alignment for a principal-coach partnership must be a priority for phase 2 as the partners establish goals, determine action steps, and extend learning for all shareholders. This phase includes three critical components. To maximize their efforts, principals and coaches must work together to (1) write shared instructional goals, (2) create a partnership plan, and (3) build capacity to empower teacher leaders.

Partners Write Shared Instructional Goals

Partners spend phase 1 establishing role clarity. Phase 2 extends the partners' work to establishing goal clarity. Role clarity is associated with a supported and functional partnership that directly benefits instructional goals (McAdam, 2023). Researcher Michael Fullan and international consultant and speaker Joanne Quinn (2016) explore the common practice that hampers schools' abilities to meet their goals: "The problem is not the absence of goals in schools and districts today but the presence of too many that are ad hoc, unconnected, and ever-changing" (p. 19). For a principal and coach to work together successfully, these partners must first agree on the goal they are working to achieve. As an interdependent pair, they must *share* that goal, both functioning within their roles to leverage the influence and access these roles allow. Their discrete perspectives are essential as they align that goal with the priorities established in phase 1 and the overall mission and vision of the school.

A clear and compelling mission and vision are essential in guiding the efforts of any organization. Goals that do not align with the mission and vision of the school have little chance of creating sustained and systemic change. To ensure their goals have a fighting chance of making inroads against the myriad distractions that beset school leaders, principals and coaches must ensure that the goals speak to the moral imperative of their school's mission, and they must take the time to define the vision of what they hope to achieve. Few schools would ever create a mission that purports to serve some of the students some of the time, or create a vision that imagines marginal success from their efforts. Mission statements usually are bold pronouncements of what schools will do, while vision statements describe ideal future states. Likewise, the shared goal of the principal and coach should be bold and embrace the potential of the partners' collective efforts. Goals are critical to determining a course of action and understanding whether those actions contribute to the desired outcomes. Author Patrick Lencioni (2012) summarizes the need for goals:

> There is no getting around the fact that the only measure of a great team—or a great organization—is whether it accomplishes what it sets out to accomplish. . . . When it comes to how a cohesive team measures its performance, one criterion sets it apart from non-cohesive ones: its goals are shared across the entire team. (pp. 65–66)

We, the authors of this book, are lucky enough to work in a school that asserts our commitment to act as a professional learning community (PLC) dedicated to ensuring high levels of learning for all. In drafting our shared goals, we needed to revisit our mission and vision to ensure that our goals were ambitious enough to help our school realize the guiding principles of our work.

To create a strong shared goal, partners should check the integrity of their goal before committing to the action steps: Is the goal valid? Is it worthy of their best efforts and collective expertise? Will the goal move the school closer to the ideal future state? Will it drive concrete, viable actions that fall within the scope of their influence and access? Goals may change over time and reflect the exigencies of the specific school year, student population, or staff capacity, but they must always hearken back to the mission of why the school exists and the vision that shareholders have for what they want the school to be.

In our work, we use the SMART criteria for writing goals: Is the goal *strategic and specific*, *measurable*, *attainable*, *results oriented*, and *time bound* (Conzemius & O'Neill, 2014)? Figures 2.1 and 2.2 (page 32) show how a principal and coach might collaborate to create a SMART goal at the elementary and secondary levels. Notice how the process begins with grounding conversation in the school's mission and coaching priorities to ensure that the goal connects directly to the broader vision of the school. Each example illustrates how specific evidence (baseline data for student reading comprehension or ACT benchmarks) drives the measurable component of the goal. The attainable and time-bound sections demonstrate how milestones are used to maintain momentum and make adjustments as needed. As you review these examples, consider how your context might require different checkpoints and data sources to achieve your goal. The key takeaway is that principals and coaches strengthen their partnership by cocreating the goal, ensuring clarity and shared ownership.

Part 1: With your partner, review the school's mission and coaching priorities.

School's Mission:

Our mission is to empower every student to reach their full potential through a caring, supportive, and collaborative learning environment where all staff work together to ensure success for all.

Coaching Priorities:

- *Improve reading comprehension in grades K–2 through small-group instruction.*
- *Increase teacher effectiveness in using common formative assessments to plan differentiated lessons.*

Part 2: Considering your answers from part 1, discuss the components of the SMART goal process in the space provided.

Strategic and Specific:

- What are we hoping to improve? (Select one of our coaching priorities.)
  Improve reading comprehension in grades K–2 through small-group instruction.
- What outcome or behavior change are we targeting?
  Teachers will implement differentiated small-group instruction focused on comprehension strategies at least three times a week.

Measurable:

- What is our current status?
  Only 40 percent of first and second graders meet grade-level reading comprehension expectations.
- What are we hoping to achieve?
  We want to increase the percentage of first and second graders meeting grade-level expectations to 70 percent by the end of the year.
- How will we monitor progress?
  - *We will review common formative assessment data every other week in our team meetings.*
  - *We will complete instructional learning walks during the English language arts block.*

Attainable:

- If we meet our goal, what will success look like?
  Teachers will consistently implement effective small-group instruction, and students' reading comprehension levels will improve.
- Are there milestones for us to measure as we are working toward the goal?
  - *By the end of the first trimester, teachers will receive professional development on differentiation and small-group reading strategies.*
  - *By the end of the second trimester, teachers will consistently implement small-group instruction at least three times a week.*

Figure 2.1: *Tool for establishing a shared instructional SMART goal—Elementary example.*

continued →

Results Oriented:

- Will this goal lead to meaningful change in teaching practices and student outcomes?

  Consistent small-group instruction will ensure targeted support for students' needs, leading to improved comprehension.
- What evidence will show the goal's impact?
  - *Student performance on formative assessments will increase.*
  - *End-of-year assessment data will show 70 percent of students meeting grade-level expectations.*

Time Bound:

- What is the timeline for achieving this goal?

  The end of the academic year
- What are the checkpoints along the way?
  - *Collaborative team check-ins to review progress*
  - *A midyear review to adjust instructional strategies if needed*

Part 3: Write a shared instructional goal.

By the end of the year, first- and second-grade teachers will implement differentiated small-group reading instruction focused on comprehension strategies at least three times per week, which will result in 70 percent of students meeting grade-level expectations.

Visit ***go.SolutionTree.com/leadership*** *for a free reproducible version of this figure.*

Part 1: With your partner, review the school's mission and coaching priorities.

School's Mission:

We are a positive and purposeful learning community dedicated to ensuring high levels of learning for all.

Coaching Priorities:

- *Strengthen the work of our collaborative teams through the use of SMART goals.*
- *Improve classroom management for struggling teachers.*
- *Increase the use of content literacy strategies in Tier 1 instruction.*

Part 2: Considering your answers from part 1, discuss the components of the SMART goal process in the space provided.

Strategic and Specific:

- What are we hoping to improve? (Select one of our coaching priorities.)

  Strengthen the work of our collaborative teams through the use of SMART goals.
- What outcome or behavior change are we targeting?

  Collaborative teams will be clear about their work and continually monitor their progress, ensuring learning for all students.

Measurable:

- What is our current status?
  Last school year, four of the thirteen core content teams met their team SMART goal.
- What are we hoping to achieve?
  One hundred percent of our core content teams will meet their team SMART goal.
- How will we monitor progress?
  We can improve our practices by collecting data during collaborative team meetings, listening to facilitator and team reflections during instructional leadership team meetings, and monitoring College Equipped Readiness Tool (CERT) assessment data.

Attainable:

- If we meet our goal, what will success look like?
  The number of students meeting benchmarks on the CERT assessment will increase in all content areas.
- Are there milestones for us to measure as we are working toward the goal?
  - *August: Teams will set a SMART goal after reviewing baseline data from the fall CERT assessment.*
  - *October: Team facilitators will provide updates during the instructional leadership team meeting.*
  - *December: Fifty percent of teams will meet the SMART goal on the winter CERT assessment.*
  - *February: Team facilitators will provide updates during the instructional leadership team meeting.*
  - *April: One hundred percent of teams will meet the SMART goal on the spring ACT or CERT assessment.*

Results Oriented:

- Will this goal lead to meaningful change in teaching practices and student outcomes?
  Yes, this aligns with our school's mission and will ensure all students are prepared for the ACT.
- What evidence will show the goal's impact?
  The number of students meeting the postsecondary readiness benchmarks will increase.

Time Bound:

- What is the timeline for achieving this goal?
  The end of the school year
- What are the checkpoints along the way?
  Weekly check-ins with collaborative teams, monthly check-ins with team facilitators, and three CERT benchmark assessments

---

Part 3: Write a shared instructional goal.

By the end of the school year, 100 percent of the core content collaborative teams will set and meet team SMART goals, resulting in increased student performance on the CERT benchmark and ACT assessments.

Figure 2.2: *Tool for establishing a shared instructional SMART goal—Secondary example.*

Partners Create a Partnership Plan

A successful principal-coach partnership plan operates within the larger context of a professional learning plan, but it is important to differentiate between these two entities. A professional learning plan is a bigger effort that includes elements of required professional development, many of which may not fall within the confines of the shared instructional goal for the principal-coach partnership. For example, a school's professional learning plan might include district-mandated training on a new language service system, annual safety compliance videos, and cyberbullying workshops. While valuable and necessary, many of these sessions are not directly tied to the partners' instructional goal. In contrast, the partnership might include a specific priority to improve schoolwide literacy practices, outlining how the principal and coach will support teacher teams to implement agreed-on strategies, review student results, and adjust instruction as needed. Instructional coaches should have a role in developing and implementing professional learning within the school, but it cannot solely be their responsibility. Creating a plan specific to the principal-coach partnership allows principals and coaches to distinguish between the requirements for whole-school professional learning and the narrowed focus of their shared instructional goal.

A partnership plan should embrace a shared instructional goal and outline the steps that the partners will take to achieve that goal. When partners write SMART goals together, they will be drafting action steps, assigning responsibilities, establishing timelines, and identifying evidence of effectiveness, which will foster greater clarity and increase the likelihood of achieving desired outcomes. Additionally, it will promote leadership capacity through reflection, collaboration, and a focused emphasis on academic goals (Bahrami, Heidari, & Cranney, 2022).

To ensure that you are maximizing your collaborative time, you must purposefully address every part of the partnership plan, including:

- Choosing data to monitor goals
- Identifying specific action steps
- Fostering ongoing reflection and making adjustments
- Celebrating progress

We discuss each of these steps in more detail in the following sections.

Choosing Data to Monitor Goals

Principals and coaches encounter hundreds of different data points each week. Without continued focus on their shared goal, they could very easily become preoccupied with data collection and lose sight of what the data is supposed to inform.

The deluge of data that confronts them requires that the principal-coach partnership agree on the metrics that matter. To monitor their shared goals, partners must agree on what data they will collect, at what intervals, and to what end. That is why the first step in the partnership plan is to determine the data you will monitor. The data you choose sets the foundation for every action step, timeline, and measure of progress that follows.

We urge principals and coaches to be selective regarding the student learning data they use to indicate progress toward their instructional SMART goals. To achieve our objectives, we emphasize the same four data criteria that we expect our teacher teams to focus on.

1. The data we choose demonstrates our commitment to a guaranteed and viable curriculum.
2. The data we choose applies across all team content and grade levels.
3. The data we choose reflects various intervals of instruction and student progress over time.
4. The data we choose is easily accessible so that time spent on data collection and management doesn't outweigh its usefulness.

For example, if the shared SMART goal focuses on improving students' ability to support claims with evidence in writing, the principal, coach, and teacher teams might administer a common writing task in courses where writing is taught. The teacher teams would score students using a shared rubric and submit a summary of the results. This process could be repeated throughout the year to spot trends across grade levels and content areas.

The data that principals and coaches choose to monitor for their SMART goals certainly isn't the only data that will inform their efforts throughout the year. Still, partners must reach a consensus on the data driving their *shared* goal. We urge partners to put as much time into carefully choosing their data sources as they put into crafting their action steps, and to invest time and space for teacher leaders to become familiar with their chosen data parameters. One strategy for selecting data sources is the partnership plan data-vetting tool, shown in figures 2.3 (page 36) and 2.4 (page 36). You and your partner can use this tool to review various data sources and determine how they inform your shared instructional SMART goal.

The data-vetting tool allows the principal and coach to analyze their current datasets and think about ways to monitor the progress of their SMART goal. This will help them as they begin to plan specific action steps toward their shared SMART goal.

Directions: With your partner, discuss and review various data sources and how they inform your shared instructional SMART goal.

Shared Instructional SMART Goal:

By the end of the year, first- and second-grade teachers will implement differentiated small-group reading instruction focused on comprehension strategies at least three times per week, which will result in 70 percent of students meeting grade-level expectations.

Potential Data Sources:

- What types of data could we collect or generate to best support our SMART goal? (Examples include formative or end-of-unit assessments, district benchmarks, teacher reflections, classroom observations, student surveys, and state or provincial assessments.)
  - *Professional development attendance data*
  - *Professional development feedback responses*
  - *Coaching calendars*
  - *Learning walk data*
  - *Monthly data analysis protocols from first- and second-grade team meetings*
  - *Coaching conversation teacher survey results*
  - *State assessment data*

Existing Data Inventory:

- What data do we *currently* have that informs our SMART goal planning? (Examples include student assessments, learning walk data, staff surveys, and student work samples.)
  - *State assessment data (from last year)*
  - *Learning walk data (from last year)*
- Based on our answers to the previous questions, what data sources will we use to track our progress?
  - *Learning walk data*
  - *Monthly data analysis protocols from first- and second-grade team meetings*

Figure 2.3: *Partnership plan data-vetting tool—Elementary example.*

Visit ***go.SolutionTree.com/leadership*** *for a free reproducible version of this figure.*

Directions: With your partner, discuss and review various data sources and how they inform your shared instructional SMART goal.

Shared Instructional SMART Goal:

By May, 100 percent of our priority collaborative teams will meet their district benchmark SMART goal.

Potential Data Sources:

- What types of data could we collect or generate to best support our SMART goal? (Examples include formative or end-of-unit assessments,

district benchmarks, teacher reflections, classroom observations, student surveys, and state or provincial assessments.)
- *Team SMART goals*
- *District benchmark data*
- *Team data analysis protocols*

Existing Data Inventory:

- What data do we *currently* have that informs our SMART goal planning? (Examples include student assessments, learning walk data, staff surveys, and student work samples.)
  District benchmark data (from last year)
- Based on our answers to the previous questions, what data sources will we use to track our progress?
  - *Team SMART goals*
  - *District benchmark data*
  - *Team data analysis protocols*

Figure 2.4: *Partnership plan data-vetting tool—Secondary example.*

Identifying Specific Action Steps

Coach Brown and Principal Jones, our principal-coach partnership from the opening scenario, know that if they are going to realize the school's mission and vision, they have no time to waste. The urgent needs of running a school may be distracting, but they must purposefully structure their time together to focus on high-leverage activities that speak to their shared goals. Using the SMART goal format will help them connect each action step to a measurable outcome and ensure they are accountable for their individual responsibilities within specified time frames.

When crafting the partnership plan, Principal Jones and Coach Brown must consider the time they will dedicate to each task. It does little good to commit to action steps that neither partner has the capacity to ensure in real time. In this moment, partners must be honest with each other and themselves about the professional learning and coaching commitments outside the partnership plan. The partnership plan is critical to the work of the principal and coach, but it is not the sum total of their responsibilities for providing feedback and support to teachers. Timelines must accurately reflect their capacities and capabilities, or else partners will quickly become frustrated and abandon even the best-laid plans.

We have found that our most effective practices involve tailoring coaching to the distinct needs of our teachers and teacher teams and their individual levels of expertise, grade levels, and teaching contexts. This differentiated approach to coaching fosters personalized professional development, which education researchers Linda Darling-Hammond, Maria E. Hyler, and Madelyn Gardner (2017) describe as "structured professional learning that results in changes in teacher practices and improvements in student learning outcomes" (p. v). It's important to recognize that action steps will change from partner to partner, from goal to goal, and from year to year. However, they should consistently reflect best practices in coaching teachers and teacher teams, while also building the capacity of teacher leaders.

We recommend the following process for identifying action steps in the partnership plan.

1. Start with the shared SMART goal.
2. Break the goal into specific actions with set timelines.
3. Assign responsibilities.
4. Define evidence of effectiveness.

To ensure they achieve their action steps, partners should regularly reflect on their progress and make adjustments as needed.

Fostering Ongoing Reflection and Making Adjustments

Even the best-laid plans require close monitoring and adjustments. Formative data collected at regular intervals allows partners to reflect on the impact of their choices and design the adjustments and interventions to get them where they want to be. The partnership plan should always include a designated time for reflection and somewhere to document needed adjustments.

For a principal-coach partnership to truly be effective, it must adhere to the same iterative progress-monitoring cycles that the partners expect their teachers to embrace as best practice for ensuring learning. Reflection is a critical component of the action plan and mirrors the work coaches do as they extend learning to teachers and teams. Knight (2022) asserts, "Coaches who work from the principle of reflection empower teachers to think deeply about what has happened in the past, what is happening in the present, and what will happen in the future" (p. 29).

For example, if a partnership plan identifies a SMART goal of improving reading comprehension by increasing the use of annotation and close readings in class, partners might review student work samples and find that annotations are mostly surface-level. They could adjust by providing additional professional learning opportunities for teachers, creating shared tools for assessing quality annotations, and establishing coaching and feedback loops to support teachers as they are refining their practice.

Partners can follow a simple cycle for fostering reflection and making adjustments in part 2 of the partnership plan.

- Schedule time to reflect and review progress toward goals.
- Examine data.
- Discuss current barriers.
- Make adjustments and record revisions.

Along the way, partners should make time to celebrate their progress. This is an essential practice, and one that partners need to be intentional about.

Celebrating Progress

Principal Jones never quite makes it to the celebration phase of the programs she initiates. She is too busy to plan an event or to think about how she might honor the work of the teachers and teams in her school. Celebration seems like a luxury she just doesn't have time for, and quite frankly, she questions why anyone would want to celebrate when they still have so far to go. For someone who is literally all over the place, she never finds herself in a place where she thanks faculty and staff or acknowledges their hard work to ensure all students learn. Coach Brown recognizes that the school's culture values hard work; however, he wonders why it also doesn't value hard workers.

To build a sustainable model of school improvement, leaders must prioritize celebrating achievements. Neglecting to celebrate progress in the interest of time management is a false economy. In reality, Principal Jones doesn't have time *not* to celebrate progress if she wants to build the culture that will support the challenging work she is asking of her faculty and staff. While celebrations of progress can and should happen in every facet of a school's culture, principals and coaches must harness the power of celebration to build and sustain the work they have dedicated themselves to in their partnership plan. That work depends on building teachers' collective efficacy to lead the work within their teams, and it requires that teachers have confidence in their ability to make instructional decisions that will help more students learn more of the time.

Educators Angela Lumpkin, Heather Claxton, and Amanda Wilson (2014) state that "by celebrating the learning of each teacher and student and the outcome of continuous educational improvement, the self-esteem of teacher leaders is reaffirmed, and teachers' motivation to teach and lead is celebrated" (p. 65). This is why we recommend that partners document their celebration in part 3 of the partnership plan framework; this ensures that recognition is built into the plan and not just an afterthought.

Celebrating teachers and their work can take many forms, from sending birthday cards to intentionally setting aside time each week to write positive notes for those working toward their goals. Like any other initiative, teacher celebrations can range from subtle individual gestures to large-scale planned events.

A popular celebration at our school was directly related to the SMART goals that each collaborative team set for student achievement on the district semester test. Our plan was simple but had a significant impact. We organized a "red carpet" event for every team that met the SMART goal they established in September. Teachers walked the red carpet during the event while students from our visual arts program took photos. Additionally, they enjoyed a lunch provided by one of our community partners. We printed certificates to honor the teachers and acknowledge their work to achieve their goals. Although it took some planning, the positive impact of the celebration was well worth the effort.

The partnership plan worksheet organizes the commitments of principals and coaches. Teams should recognize that this document is dynamic, displaying the team's initial commitments as well as the reflective activity that may shift the team's work over time. Figure 2.5 (page 42) shows how a team at the elementary level might complete this worksheet, and figure 2.6 (page 44) shows an example at the secondary level.

Working through the partnership plan is a multifaceted, dynamic process that will require partners to lean into their work from phase 1. They will need to rely on their norms to ensure they are valuing the person *and* the work, and they will need to revisit what they consider most important about their time together. Partners should make time to celebrate the successes of not just the people they lead but one another as well. Ultimately, for a partnership plan to be successful, the relationship must be successful, and that means honoring the journey you are on together.

The Partnership Perspective

PRINCIPAL AND COACH INSIGHTS

PRINCIPAL PERSPECTIVE: *Rebecca*

As I started this work, I would feel restless and twitchy whenever I had to sit down and spend time on something that felt abstract. Goals were things that we documented for our yearly required school-improvement plan, not things that governed my daily decision-making process or calendar commitments. I operated under a belief system that probably looked like "the more things, the better," and most of my actions were scattershot at best, informed by best intentions but definitely not best practice. Celebrations were to be saved for another day—a day when I wasn't so busy putting out fires. To become a better principal, I had to embrace a shared goal made concrete with actionable steps.

The SMART goals we set as a partnership keep our time focused on high-yield strategies. Our partnership plan allows us to see the trajectory of our work over time. I finally feel like my need for constant motion has a mission—ensuring learning for all students in our school.

COACH PERSPECTIVE: Brittany

I have always found joy in celebrating and have recently found myself on a journey of learning more about what it truly means to celebrate intentionally. Celebrating can mean delivering birthday cards, writing positive notes, or surprising coworkers with breakfast or lunch. Celebrating can also include recognizing growth in a specific area, acknowledging the significant accomplishment of meeting a goal, or noting when a team comes together and completes a task collaboratively.

I have learned that celebration comes down to two things: (1) relationships and (2) routine. To celebrate well, we have to take the time to get to know the people around us, and we have to prioritize celebrating daily. I am learning how to make celebration a daily routine by using my calendar, setting reminders, and organizing my desk so I make celebrating a priority. I am continuing to learn how each educator in our building contributes to our school's mission. The journey of learning how to celebrate is ongoing, but I know that committing to celebrate the students and educators I work with every day will have an impact.

Partners Build Capacity to Empower Teacher Leaders

To sustain the improvement efforts envisioned in the partnership plan and to ensure that the responsibility for adult learning does not rest solely on the principal's and coach's shoulders, the partners must commit to building teacher and team capacity for the work. The partnership plan must support teachers and teacher teams because the objective of the plan is to create widely dispersed leadership and ownership of school-improvement goals. Academic and author Linda Lambert (2002) finds "the old model of formal, one-person leadership leaves the substantial

Team Members: *Strong (principal), Washington (instructional coach), and Scott (reading interventionist)*

School Mission: *We are a nurturing and inclusive environment dedicated to ensuring all students achieve academic success and develop strong character.*

Coaching Priority:

- *Improve reading comprehension in grades K–2 through small-group instruction.*
- *Increase teacher effectiveness in using common formative assessments to plan differentiated lessons.*

Coaching Goal: *By the end of the year, first- and second-grade teachers will implement differentiated small-group reading instruction focused on comprehension strategies at least three times per week, which will result in 70 percent of students meeting grade-level expectations.*

Part 1: Action Steps

Strategies and Action Steps	Principal Responsibility	Coach Responsibility	Timeline	Evidence of Effectiveness
Attend district professional development on small-group reading instruction.	*Invite first- and second-grade teacher leaders to attend professional development. Attend professional development with the school team.*	*Attend professional development.*	*July*	*Teachers will use implementation logs demonstrating the use of small-group reteaching.*
Create a schedule for job-embedded professional development focused on small-group reading instruction and comprehension strategies.	*With district coaches, coordinate dates and times for professional development. Communicate with teachers about the importance of and need for this specific professional development.*	*Reserve space and send invites to teachers for professional development. Arrange coverage for teachers for during-the-day trainings.*	*August*	*Teachers will use a calendar of scheduled sessions and attendance records.*
Ensure access to resources.	*Work with an ordering and receiving clerk to purchase supplies for small-group instruction.*	*Work with teachers and district coaches to create a list of requested supplies (furniture, manipulatives, and so on).*	*July to August*	*Teachers will have access to the requested resources by the middle of September.*
Model and co-teach with teachers.	*Schedule time to reflect with the instructional coach.*	*Schedule times to model and co-teach with first- and second-grade teachers.*	*August to September*	*Instructional coaches will model and co-teach with every first- and second-grade teacher at least once by the end of September.*

Support teacher teams with data analysis and planning for small-group instruction.	*Attend weekly team meetings with the instructional coach. Track when data discussions occur using a data-collection tool.*	*Attend weekly team meetings with the principal. Meet with team leads for twice-monthly check-ins.*	*August to April*	*Teams will have at least one data discussion per month, after which they plan specific action steps.*
Conduct walkthroughs during small-group reading instruction and provide specific and positive feedback.	*Conduct walkthroughs with the instructional coach.*	*Schedule walkthroughs. Conduct walkthroughs with the principal.*	*September to April*	*All first- and second-grade teachers will receive specific and positive feedback about small-group reading instruction at least one time per month.*
Conduct four-week coaching cycles with individual teachers.	*Conduct twice-monthly coaching conversations with the instructional coach.*	*Schedule coaching cycles. Send preobservation, observation, and postobservation calendar invites.*	*October to April*	*All first- and second-grade teachers will complete at least one four-week coaching cycle with the instructional coach.*

Part 2: Reflections and Adjustments

When will we take time to reflect on and monitor the progress of our action steps?

September 13, November 13, January 15, March 19, May 7

According to our data, what adjustments do we need to make to meet our SMART goal? *No adjustments needed at this time.*

Part 3: Celebrations

How will we celebrate when action steps are accomplished?

- *We will highlight teacher practices in the morning email and at weekly faculty meetings.*
- *We will celebrate teams for having data discussions by bringing cupcakes to their next meeting.*
- *We will write a positive note to each teacher at the end of every coaching cycle.*
- *We will celebrate by having lunch together every time we complete an action step.*

How will we celebrate when we meet our shared SMART goal?

- *We will have a luncheon for leadership and first- and second-grade teams.*
- *We will apply to present our work at a national conference.*

Source: Adapted from DuFour et al., 2024.

Figure 2.5: *Partnership plan worksheet—Elementary example.*

*Visit **go.SolutionTree.com/leadership** for a free reproducible version of this figure.*

Team Members: *Rebecca Nicolas (principal), Michelle Marrillia (instructional coach), and Brittany Mozingo (instructional coach)*
School Mission: *We are a positive and purposeful learning community dedicated to ensuring high levels of learning for all.*
Coaching Priority: *Collaborative teams*
Coaching Goal: *By May, 100 percent of our priority collaborative teams will meet their district benchmark SMART goal.*

Part 1: Action Steps

Strategies and Action Steps	Principal Responsibility	Coach Responsibility	Timeline	Evidence of Effectiveness
Plan professional development for SMART goal creation.	*Review, approve, and support the professional development plan.*	*Design a professional development plan and submit it to the principal.* *Create a coaching schedule.*	*September 6*	*Complete and implement the professional development plan.*
Support collaborative teams as they are creating their SMART goal.	*Attend collaborative team meetings.* *Ensure assistant principals attend the meetings.*	*Attend and provide support during collaborative team meetings.*	*Week of September 16*	*Each collaborative team will create a SMART goal.*
Provide feedback on SMART goals.	*Schedule an administrator-coach meeting.*	*Facilitate an administrator-coach meeting.*	*Week of September 23*	*Every team will have an approved SMART goal with action steps.*
Schedule facilitator check-ins.	*Create one to three reflection questions to discuss with team leaders.*	*Create one to three reflection questions to discuss with team leaders.* *Schedule coaching conversations with team leaders.* *Meet individually with team leaders.*	*October 21 and November 11*	*Team leaders will lead planning discussions with collaborative teams.*

Create a schoolwide communication plan (before Thanksgiving).	*Provide feedback on a slide deck.* *Provide daily morning announcements.* *Create motivational videos for students.*	*Create a shared slide deck for each department to support skills and test-taking strategies.*	*Presentation to team leads on November 11* *Presentation to students on November 25*	*All students taking benchmark assessments will hear common messaging.*
Create a schoolwide incentive plan.	*Promote student engagement through the morning announcements and discuss strategies with collaborative teams.*	*Work with the culture and climate leads to plan for the incentive event.*	*Informational flyer ready to present by November 11* *Event on December 19*	*The celebration event will take place on December 19.*

Part 2: Reflections and Adjustments

When will we take time to reflect on and monitor the progress of our action steps?

September 18, October 14, November 15, December 13

According to our data, what adjustments do we need to make to meet our SMART goal?

No adjustment needed at this time.

Part 3: Celebrations

- How will we celebrate when action steps are accomplished?
  - *Team leaders will receive positive notes after the October 21 and November 11 check-ins to highlight celebrations and progress their teams have had.*
  - *We will hold a schoolwide celebration in December to celebrate students meeting benchmarks, students showing significant improvement, and collaborative teams meeting their SMART goal.*
- How will we celebrate when we meet our shared SMART goal?
  - *Teams will be invited to an end-of-year reception with cake and awards.*
  - *We will schedule a fancy dinner for our team.*

Source: Adapted from DuFour et al., 2024.

Figure 2.6: *Partnership plan worksheet—Secondary example.*

talents of teachers largely untapped." Improvements achieved under this model are not easy to sustain. Our mission commits to high levels of learning for all. When that *all* includes teachers, we can ensure that student learning is supported by a network of adult learners working toward the same goals.

To ensure you are aligned in the work of your partnership, you must commit to supporting individual teachers, supporting teacher teams, and developing teacher leaders.

Supporting Individual Teachers

To gain real traction with their partnership plan goals, Principal Jones must recognize that Coach Brown's job is to coach. According to Jim Knight (2024):

> When coaches focus on capacity building, there are tasks that they do not do. Usually, coaches do not sub when teachers are away, do administrative work, or work directly with students except in the service of the larger goal of promoting teacher growth.

To create a professional learning culture, coaches should spend most of their time with teachers. Coach Brown must protect his time and remind his principal of their shared goals as they move through phase 2. He will work with individual teachers, giving veteran teachers support and feedback as they navigate the new expectations of a changing culture and providing new teachers with structure and guidance as they acclimate to their position and the school.

Darling-Hammond and colleagues (2017) assert, "Professional development models associated with gains in student learning frequently provide built-in time for teachers to think about, receive input on, and make changes to their practice" (p. 14). To best serve our individual teachers, our coaches created a teacher academy, where targeted teachers were invited to participate and learn with a cohort of like-minded peers. Teachers received individualized feedback from coaches but also had the opportunity to learn from one another as they each pursued improvement priorities that reflected their needs. The cohort focused on acquiring leadership skills and encouraged individual teachers to think about their role in the school and how they could best cultivate a leadership perspective to move the school forward.

You can replicate this model in your own school by doing the following.

- **Identifying the focus group:** Select teachers whose professional growth priorities align with the school's instructional goals or who would benefit from targeted support.
- **Creating a cohort:** Schedule meetings where teachers will collaborate, learn, and reflect together.

- **Building in time for feedback:** Ensure that teachers receive individualized coaching support and time for peer-to-peer learning.

With clear goals and built-in feedback, a teacher academy provides a structured pathway for meaningful teacher professional learning.

Supporting Teacher Teams

As educators dedicated to working as a collaborative team, we know that teacher teams are critical to the work of school improvement and that, as educator John D'Auria (2015) asserts, "the ability to develop and support high-functioning teams schoolwide is essential to ensuring improved and inspired learning for all learners—adults or children" (p. 54). The partnership plan should capitalize on the work of teams to build capacity for the collaborative work that will ensure a guaranteed and viable curriculum. In their book *Amplify Your Impact*, Thomas W. Many, Michael J. Maffoni, Susan K. Sparks, and Tesha Ferriby Thomas (2018) concisely explain that, "if coaching individuals is good, then coaching collaborative teams is better" (p. 7).

There are no shortcuts to spending time with teachers as they do the work of ensuring quality instruction. Principals and coaches must regularly attend teacher team meetings to support the teams with embedded feedback and coaching. In those meetings, coaches can model how to determine essential learning targets or assist a struggling team with a data protocol to analyze student work. Principals might ask clarifying questions that connect the team's work to schoolwide goals or highlight evidence of effectiveness. These small but intentional actions help teams stay focused, learn together, and build shared ownership.

However, it is critical that neither coaches nor principals attempt to lead teacher meetings. When this happens, very often, the meetings become mini faculty meetings, with teachers listening to the person in charge rather than collaborating with one another as team members. The responsibility for leading meetings should go to a teacher leader who is trained in the process and adept at managing adult learners while still functioning as an active team member. This is not always an easy space for prospective teacher leaders; many will need training and support to adapt to the role. Coaches are uniquely positioned to help teacher leaders develop their leadership acumen and focus on achieving team goals. Over time, this approach builds teacher leaders' confidence and skill, enabling the principal and coach to step back as the team capacity grows.

Developing Teacher Leaders

Teacher team leaders are a critical bridge between the work of the principal and coach and the work of the teacher teams. Researchers Jianping Shen, Huang Wu, Patricia Reeves, Yunzheng Zheng, Lisa Ryan, and Dustin Anderson (2020) find that teacher leadership has a positive relationship with student achievement. We have found that investing in the development and support of teacher leaders pays significant dividends down the line as we help teams. At our school, we call our teacher team leaders *facilitators* and emphasize that their primary task is facilitating adult learning. They are not department chairs or supervisors. They help create the conditions so they can learn, along with their team, and improve their instructional practice with the goal of achieving greater student achievement.

We build strong relationships with our facilitators, as they are the key to our vision of widely dispersed leadership. We have found that the best facilitators are not always the most veteran teachers on the team; teachers in their third or fourth year of practice seem inclined to treat team meetings less like mini department meetings and more like collaborative units. However, we know that all our facilitators need support and coaching as they inhabit the complex role of facilitator. Weekly coaching check-ins help facilitators craft agendas, troubleshoot team challenges, and procure resources for their team's work.

Principals and coaches must be dedicated to learning along with teachers, teams, and facilitators. As Knight (2022) asserts, "When coaches have an authentic, humble desire to learn from teachers, see and affirm teachers' strengths, and demonstrate that they truly have teachers' best interest at heart, teachers are more likely to engage fully in coaching" (p. 73). The same applies to developing teacher leaders; when we invest in their professional growth, we strengthen their leadership, and ultimately their entire team.

In addition to supporting individual teachers and teacher teams, your partnership should reflect on how you are developing teacher leaders. This ongoing reflection helps you track what is working and when and how to make adjustments and will ultimately strengthen capacity across all three areas.

The tool in figure 2.7 is designed for partners to move beyond reflection into action. By taking time to document your current practices and identify areas for improvement, you create a clear record of how to support individual teachers, teacher teams, and team leaders. We suggest revisiting this tool once or twice per semester to track progress, adjust accordingly, and celebrate wins along the way.

Directions: With your partner, discuss and review successful teacher and team supports and how they enhance instruction. After completing the review, highlight new practices that will directly impact your team's shared SMART goal and determine which current practices you should adjust or eliminate.

	Successful Current Practices	**Potential New Practices**	**Practices to Adjust or Eliminate**
Supporting individual teachers	• *New teacher mentoring with classroom support* • *Targeted professional development on classroom management*	• *Facilitate peer observations with structured reflections.*	• *Streamline or eliminate excessive documentation that pulls from instruction.*
Supporting teacher teams	• *PLC dashboard to organize team meetings*	• *Provide support on establishing success criteria for essential learning targets.*	• *Replace roundtable sharing of anecdotes with a data protocol using common assessment results and student work samples.*
Developing teacher leaders	• *Weekly coaching check-ins* • *PLC dashboard templates and tools for team meetings* • *Facilitator weekly communication slide deck* • *Leadership book study*	• *Launch peer observation rounds between facilitators.*	• *Replace the standing facilitator monthly meeting with targeted needs-based sessions.*

Figure 2.7: *Building teacher and team capacity reflection tool.*

Visit ***go.SolutionTree.com/leadership*** *for a free reproducible version of this figure.*

Calibration Conversations

The calibration conversations for this phase allow you to grapple with common scenarios that may stall you and your partner's productivity. Whether you are challenged by building shared instructional goals or choosing meaningful data to monitor the progress of school-improvement initiatives, the scenarios encourage you to examine how your current practices support your efforts. Read each scenario and imagine it playing out in your own context. How would you react if this were your partnership? Use the read, react, and reflect protocol in figure 2.8 to compare your own practices to those in the scenarios and identify ways to strengthen your work together.

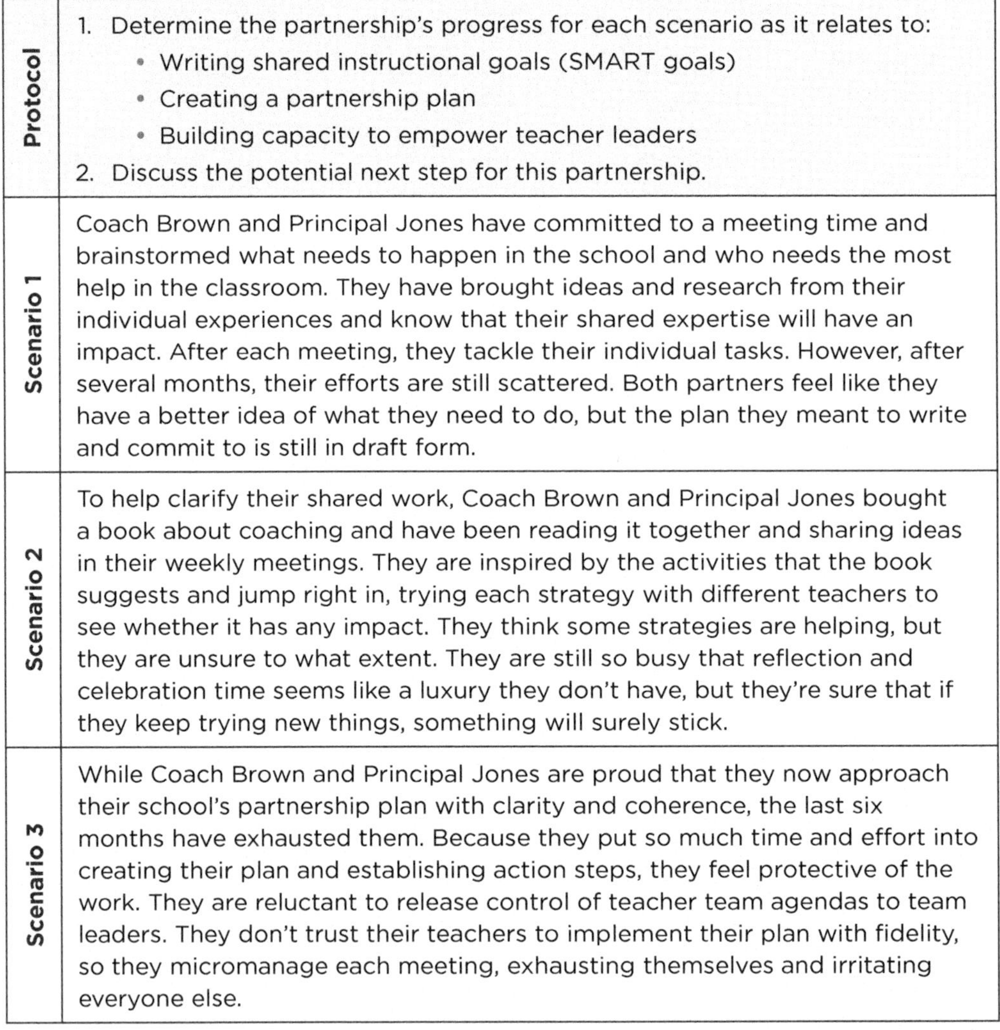

Protocol	1. Determine the partnership's progress for each scenario as it relates to: • Writing shared instructional goals (SMART goals) • Creating a partnership plan • Building capacity to empower teacher leaders 2. Discuss the potential next step for this partnership.
Scenario 1	Coach Brown and Principal Jones have committed to a meeting time and brainstormed what needs to happen in the school and who needs the most help in the classroom. They have brought ideas and research from their individual experiences and know that their shared expertise will have an impact. After each meeting, they tackle their individual tasks. However, after several months, their efforts are still scattered. Both partners feel like they have a better idea of what they need to do, but the plan they meant to write and commit to is still in draft form.
Scenario 2	To help clarify their shared work, Coach Brown and Principal Jones bought a book about coaching and have been reading it together and sharing ideas in their weekly meetings. They are inspired by the activities that the book suggests and jump right in, trying each strategy with different teachers to see whether it has any impact. They think some strategies are helping, but they are unsure to what extent. They are still so busy that reflection and celebration time seems like a luxury they don't have, but they're sure that if they keep trying new things, something will surely stick.
Scenario 3	While Coach Brown and Principal Jones are proud that they now approach their school's partnership plan with clarity and coherence, the last six months have exhausted them. Because they put so much time and effort into creating their plan and establishing action steps, they feel protective of the work. They are reluctant to release control of teacher team agendas to team leaders. They don't trust their teachers to implement their plan with fidelity, so they micromanage each meeting, exhausting themselves and irritating everyone else.

Figure 2.8: *Read, react, and reflect protocol.*

Final Thoughts

Even partners who have worked together for a long time need to ensure they are aligning their efforts in a systematic and purposeful way. We know that without the structure of our partnership plan, we tend to gravitate toward activities that are easy to implement or that align with our individual strengths and preferences. The partnership framework pushes us to extend beyond our comfort zones and to tackle the challenges that will have the greatest leverage as we embrace the ambitious and worthy mission to which we have committed ourselves.

We also know that we can't do the work in isolation. The principal and coach must reach beyond the parameters of the partnership to engage all the adult learners in the school. We build credibility for our efforts when we embrace a coaching culture by learning alongside teachers and teacher leaders, showing grace and patience for others as well as ourselves, and celebrating our wins.

When working with your partner, consider the actions listed in figure 2.9. Complete each action in the checklist to ensure you fully implement phase 2.

- ☐ Establish a shared instructional SMART goal (figures 2.1, page 31, and 2.2, page 32).
- ☐ Vet the data you will use for your partnership plan (figures 2.3, page 36, and 2.4, page 36).
- ☐ Create your partnership plan and commit to action steps (figures 2.5, page 42, and 2.6, page 44).
- ☐ Reflect on building teacher and team capacity (figure 2.7, page 49).
- ☐ With your partner, work through the read, react, and reflect protocol for phase 2 (figure 2.8, page 50).

Figure 2.9: *Phase 2 checklist—Establishing goals and actions.*

Visit ***go.SolutionTree.com/leadership*** *for a free reproducible version of this figure.*

Pause to Reflect II

Reflect on the following questions as you close out phase 2.

- How does your partnership currently address goals and action steps? How might establishing a shared instructional SMART goal and creating a partnership plan impact your instructional work?
- What tools does your team need to start using to support goal setting?

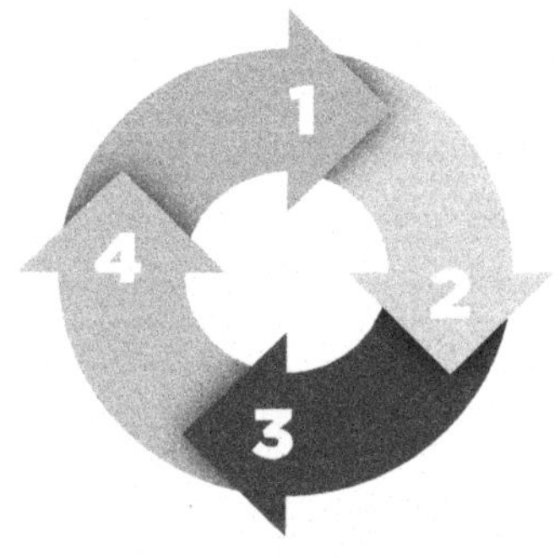

PHASE 3
Monitoring and Adjusting

- Prioritize coaching.
- Measure what matters.
- Maintain momentum.

Consider the following hypothetical scenario.

Principal Harvey and Coach Patel have worked together for two years. They agree on the needs of Madison Elementary School and have committed to norms that sustain their working relationship. They started this year with the best intentions, crafting a partnership plan with carefully delineated goals and timelines that, unfortunately, keep getting past them. District initiatives are not necessarily compatible with their goals, and seemingly, every new email, mandated training, and role-group meeting brings new distractions and additional work that does not align with the goals they committed to at their summer retreat.

Last week, Principal Harvey canceled their principal-coach meeting because he had to finish evaluation conferences. Coach Patel had to cancel this week because she was called into yet another district training on a new software platform that tracks interventions. If you asked either of them, they would attest that they are still committed to their goals, but they feel compelled to override those commitments when the *required* parts of their jobs arise. They sometimes pass in the hallway, both rushing to a different location and assuring each other that they will reschedule their meeting soon, but nothing comes of it.

Soon, two months have passed without them meeting. They haven't collected data, much less looked at it, or provided feedback to their teachers and teams. They can tell by their teacher team agendas that some teams have become mired in personal drama and don't know how to move forward, but there's no time to dig in and diagnose what is happening. For Principal Harvey, each day feels like a sprint to complete everything on his list. When the final bell rings each day, he is exhausted and a little confused about where the time has gone. Coach Patel is spending time with teachers but wonders about the impact of that time. As the school's only instructional coach, she receives every so-called instructional initiative and meeting requirement the district sends to the school. She worries about the mixed messages she sends teachers as these requirements increasingly occupy their time together. If this principal and this coach don't course-correct soon, the entire year will get away from them, but neither of them is taking the initiative to confront the situation. Who has the time for that, anyway?

Reflection Questions

Based on the preceding scenario, answer the following questions.

- What obligations distract you from your commitment to ensuring instructional priorities?
- What systems have you established for tracking progress toward your goals?
- What do you do when your team experiences setbacks?
- How do you ensure clear communication of priorities when outside initiatives distract from or conflict with your shared goals?

Principal Harvey and Coach Patel are suffering from the curse of best intentions. Despite what they intend to do, they are not holding themselves or each other accountable for the commitments they made earlier in the partnership. By failing to prioritize the work, they are ensuring that the partnership plan doesn't move beyond being just a plan. Phase 3 adds accountability structures that ensure the plan becomes reality.

Here, we'll explore the third phase of the partnership framework, where partners monitor the plan they developed in phase 2 and adjust as needed. Partners can accomplish this by prioritizing coaching, auditing their calendars, eliminating barriers to commitment, using data to inform decisions, and using accountability to maintain momentum.

Collaboration in Action: Key Moves and Essential Tools

The third phase of the partnership framework is designed to help the principal and coach stay the course. To do this, they need to (1) prioritize coaching, (2) measure what matters, and (3) maintain momentum and accountability by clearly communicating their collective commitments to both themselves and the larger school community. The key to phase 3 is intentionality. Partners must intentionally protect the time and space for the work by committing to the shared goals they identified in phase 2 and walking the walk for themselves and the school they serve.

Partners Prioritize Coaching

As principals and coaches move into phase 3, they must confront the finite resource determining whether their partnership plan is successful: time. A very valuable benefit of the partnership framework is that it allows the principal and coach to protect each other's time. Principal Harvey can ensure that his coach has the time and space to conduct the high-leverage coaching work that will move teachers forward. Coach Patel can help her principal focus on the intentionality and coherence of the school's initiatives so that he is an instructionally focused leader. To fully leverage this potential, teams must effectively manage their time to ensure the implementation of their shared goals.

We urge teams to become clear-eyed about where they are already spending their time. Calendar audits can be revelatory and help teams realign their schedules to best serve their goals and ensure learning for all. As teams move forward, they can use regular audits to ensure they are doing the work they committed to when they had time to think about the purpose of their time together. Principals need time to ensure school initiatives are coherent in their purpose and delivery; coaches need time to coach. The partnership plan is critical in ensuring two of the busiest people in the school prioritize these needs in their respective schedules.

Auditing the Coach and Principal Calendars

Every school building is different, and every coach will be tasked with different responsibilities. Principal-coach partners must assume responsibility for ensuring that the coach's time is well spent on high-leverage activities that positively influence student learning. To do this effectively, they should intentionally align coaching efforts with professional development practices that research identifies as most impactful.

Effective professional development centers on teaching strategies associated with specific curriculum content so that it supports teachers' learning within their classroom contexts (Darling-Hammond et al., 2017). The partners can maximize their impact on instructional practices and student achievement by ensuring that coaching is focused on content and grounded in discipline-specific pedagogy, rather than the myriad tasks that can crop up and monopolize a coach's time or attention.

Additionally, effective coaching should incorporate opportunities for feedback and reflection, which Darling-Hammond and colleagues (2017) describe as "[helping] teachers to thoughtfully move toward the expert visions of practice" (p. vi). Joellen Killion and Cindy Harrison (2017) further assert that "coaching, to be effective, must have a defined purpose and goal, establish clear roles for coaches to guide their daily work, and be conducted within a culture of continuous improvement" (p. 15). Considering these principles, partners can foster a structured, supportive environment that enhances teaching practices and elevates student learning outcomes.

By intentionally documenting daily activities, the principal and coach can systematically review how they spend their time. The instructional time audit tool in figure 3.1 allows the principal and coach to note emerging trends and patterns and have meaningful conversations about the effectiveness of their own schedules. Using this tool helps them ensure alignment with instructional priorities, while also maintaining the momentum needed to do meaningful work. For the coach, completing this audit means prioritizing activities that enhance teacher capacity and student outcomes. For the principal, an instructional time audit may reveal that they are spending very little time in classrooms or in front of teachers, underscoring the need to realign the schedules with high-yield instructional moves. By routinely auditing their calendars, partners can make informed decisions to prioritize activities that yield the greatest benefits and stay true to their shared goals.

Turning Insight Into Action

After completing the instructional time audit, you may be overwhelmed to see all the tasks at hand. Scheduling classroom observations, supporting teachers, attending team meetings, providing professional development, and participating in countless meetings will easily fill a principal and coach's weekly schedule. The principal or coach could easily fall into a pattern of just checking the boxes. Taking the time to do this audit can be essential to ensuring that the busyness of the day is meaningful and thoughtful work.

To make the most of the audit, we suggest the following actions.

Purpose: To review how instructional time is currently spent and prioritize activities with the greatest impact on teaching and learning

Step 1: Activities to Accomplish

First, before starting your workday, write down the essential activities that you would like to accomplish. Next, use the following table to complete a time audit. List your activities, descriptions of them, the time spent per day, and the activities' ultimate purpose.

Activity	Description	Time Spent per Day	Purpose
Team meetings	*Attend the English 2 collaborative team meeting.*	*1.5 hours*	*Team collaboration and new curriculum implementation*
Individual teacher support	*Provide technology support and do new teacher check-ins.*	*1.5 hours*	*Individual teacher support*
Learning walks	*Do Algebra 1 class visits.*	*1 hour*	*Data collection and feedback*
Lunch and hall duty	*Exchange cafeteria and class supervision.*	*1.5 hours*	*Student supervision*
Planning	*Plan for upcoming job-embedded professional development.*	*1 hour*	*Planning*
Principal-coach meeting	*Reflect on action steps and plan for the first leadership meeting.*	*1 hour*	*Reflection and planning*

Step 2: Audit Reflection

Before a meeting with your partner, review your time audit and consider the following six questions.

1. Where do you spend the majority of your time?

   The majority of my time is spent on instructionally related tasks.

2. Does your schedule currently prioritize high-impact instructional improvement (team and individual coaching, collaborative planning, teacher observations, and feedback)?

   Yes. With the exception of the 1.5 hours spent on supervision and on technology support, my tasks are teacher- and instruction-focused.

3. How closely does your schedule align with priorities outlined in phase 1? (See figure 1.2, page 31.)

   When I look at the time spent on supervision tasks over the span of a week (7.5 hours), I feel that may not completely align with our original plan.

4. What activities are currently consuming time but not directly improving instruction (for example, excessive administrative tasks, nonspecific check-ins, technology troubleshooting, or helping-hand tasks)?

   Daily lunch duty is time-consuming and also interferes with individual teacher support. Some of our teachers' assigned planning time falls during my lunch supervision time. Additionally, some teachers call me to get my help with technology instead of reaching out to tech support. This is consuming more time than I initially realized.

Figure 3.1: *Sample instructional time audit tool.*

continued →

5. Are there activities that need to be added to the calendar?
   Not at this time.
6. Are there activities that need to be avoided or abandoned?
   I would like to consider removing lunch duty from my calendar one day each week.

Step 3: Partner Discussion

After collecting data, you and your partner can use the reflection questions to determine whether you need to adjust your calendars.

Visit ***go.SolutionTree.com/leadership*** *for a free reproducible version of this figure.*

- Identify time patterns that reveal what you are prioritizing. Are you spending too much time on logistics and not enough time on teacher or team coaching?
- Compare your current use of time to your partnership SMART goal. Which activities prioritize student and teacher learning? Which activities can you delegate or eliminate?
- Make adjustments to your schedule to maximize your impact.

As our team has done this work, we have intentionally reflected on the coaching shifts that have helped us maximize our time and our impact.

Figure 3.2 provides suggestions for how principals and coaches can make simple shifts to common coaching activities in order to guide teachers and teacher teams. We suggest treating this tool as both a model and a way to reflect on your current practices. (You can record your own coaching shifts in the blank version of the figure, available online.) This process allows partners to move ideas from the audit into actionable next steps.

If you're trying to . . .	Move from this . . .	To this . . .
Build trust and rapport	The principal or coach frequently walks the hallways and offers generic praise and greetings.	The principal or coach builds trust with teachers by actively listening, clearly communicating, asking questions, and empowering teachers.
Observe classrooms	The principal or coach visits classrooms randomly without leaving feedback for the teachers.	The principal or coach frequently observes classrooms and provides teachers with actionable feedback and positive reinforcement.

Set goals	The principal or coach sets generic goals with teams and does not provide follow-up or accountability.	The principal or coach collaborates with teachers and teams to set actionable goals based on student needs and data analysis.
Provide instructional strategies	The principal or coach provides generic strategies without examples or actionable next steps.	The principal or coach offers targeted instructional strategies that address specific student needs.
Coach teams	The principal or coach attends teacher team meetings but does not actively participate.	The principal or coach attends team meetings and encourages teachers and teams to reflect on current practices, analyze data, and identify areas of improvement.
Coach individuals	The principal or coach checks in with teachers, but these interactions are often quick and unplanned.	The principal or coach intentionally plans for individual teacher coaching and uses data to drive coaching conversations.
Provide positive reinforcement and feedback	The principal or coach occasionally writes positive notes to teachers.	The principal or coach provides regular positive reinforcement and feedback to teachers to promote continuous improvement.
Provide professional development	The principal or coach provides stand-and-deliver professional development to the whole staff.	The principal or coach provides relevant, differentiated, and meaningful professional development throughout the school year.
Make meetings meaningful	The principal or coach attends all required meetings but does not actively participate or listen.	The principal or coach attends all required meetings and continually reflects on how the information will impact school goals and student learning. Following the meetings, they share action steps and communicate them to shareholders.
Document school-improvement efforts	The principal or coach completes required documentation but does so in isolation and does not seek input from shareholders.	The principal or coach collaborates with school leaders to document efforts of continuous improvement within the school.

Figure 3.2: *Coaching shift considerations.*

Visit ***go.SolutionTree.com/leadership*** *for a free reproducible version of this figure.*

Eliminating Commitment Creep

A school, like any large organization, has a number of shareholders. Each shareholder will have special interests and an agenda that serves what they believe to be the most important leverage point for positive change. For example, on any given day, principals may be asked to consider equity initiatives, culture- and climate-building activities, curriculum implementation planning, athletic schedules, building maintenance, and parent safety concerns. The instructional time audit may reveal that the principal is spending time on instructional initiatives that do not align with the school's goals and that detract them from delivering a coherent improvement plan. Coaches may be asked to take on improvement plans for struggling teachers, curriculum implementation training, or documentation for federal funding, or to track down teachers who have not completed professional development requirements. All these activities may fall within the job descriptions of these roles, and time spent on these activities may be deemed legitimate uses of these people's time and attention. However, Fullan and Quinn (2016) urge schools to focus direction: "Leaders need to find the glue that will increase the coherence of the district and school efforts at every level and build a clear path to improve learning in demonstrable ways" (p. 17). The audit tools we've discussed can ferret out the commitments that distract a principal and coach, but the challenge of having many commitments is that they all seem deserving of the principal and coach's time.

We have found it important to identify tasks that creep into our schedules and take away valuable time needed to ensure a high-impact instructional focus. This *commitment creep*, as we call it, can steal attention from the shared goals of the partnership plan. To prevent commitment creep, principal and coach must be mindful of the legitimate interests, obligations, and worthy activities that infringe on the finite resource of time. As a school year progresses, even the best-laid plans can fall by the wayside. We use the commitment creep analysis tool shown in figure 3.3 to remain focused on the right work of continuous improvement in our school.

To ensure that commitment creep does not compromise the integrity of the partnership plan, partners must be transparent and vocal about the work to which they have dedicated themselves. If shareholders do not know how the principal and coach are spending their time, they may feel that their concerns have been sidelined without understanding how and why certain work has been prioritized.

Partners Measure What Matters

The partnership framework requires partners to collect data and monitor goals to ensure actions are having the impact that the partners expect them to have. Ideally,

Step 1: Identification

Identify tasks that may be creeping into your schedule and taking away valuable time needed to ensure a high-impact instructional focus.

Commitment or Task	Why It Is Happening	Action Plan to Reduce or Delegate It
Time dedicated to emails	*I am responding to emails all day long. I lack dedicated time to read and respond to correspondence. It feels like everything is an emergency.*	*I'll limit email check-ins to scheduled times: thirty minutes each morning before school and thirty minutes midday.*
Excessive meetings	*I am pulled into meetings that do not have an instructional focus (operational tasks, committee work, and so on).*	*I'll review agendas before meetings and determine whether I must attend.*

Step 2: Accountability and Adjustment

With your partner, use the prompts from step 1 to discuss which commitments and tasks need to be adjusted to ensure that the majority of the coach's time is dedicated to high-impact coaching work. Record notes as needed in the space provided.

A discussion about shifting time commitments might go as follows.

Coach: "After analyzing my time commitments from the past week, it's become clear to me that my time spent in meetings exceeds my time spent with individual teachers. For the next two weeks, I propose that I skip the optional district office hours for the new curriculum tools. I've got a good handle on those already, and I think my time would be better spent with the seventh-grade team as they are working through the new texts."

Principal: "Are we concerned that no one from our school will be represented at those meetings?"

Coach: "Meetings are recorded and sent out afterward. If it seems like I'm missing something, I can review them later."

Figure 3.3: *Commitment creep analysis tool.*

*Visit **go.SolutionTree.com/leadership** for a free reproducible version of this figure.*

creating the partnership plan has guided them to easily gather data, provide interim updates, and make formative insights and adjustments. Committing to careful data choices earlier in the framework will pay dividends throughout the year as commitments pile up and distractions make teams feel time-starved. It is also critical that the partners' choices allow for responsible accountability. Jim Knight (2022) asserts:

> When educators are responsibly accountable, their professional learning has an unmistakable impact on student learning, making them accountable to students, parents, fellow educators, and other stakeholders. Further, at the individual or school level, responsible accountability represents a genuine commitment, both individually and collectively, to professional learning and growth—a recognition that, to have learning students, we need to also have learning teachers, learning coaches, and learning administrators. In short, responsible accountability is essential for professional learning—and it isn't possible without choice. (p. 24)

Responsible accountability is at the heart of the partnership framework. For principals and coaches, this means collecting actionable data, intentionally using that data to guide growth, and following through with actions that improve teaching and learning. The next subsections outline how to put this into practice.

Walking the Walk

While leaders and coaches may collect data in various ways, ultimately, there is no substitute for being in classrooms, learning from teachers, and observing how students are learning. Many schools conduct what are often called *learning walks*—short, focused classroom visits designed to gather evidence of teaching and learning to inform teacher growth and improvement. The process can be time-consuming, and if done without intentionality, learning walks may seem to exist so that administrators can check on teachers. In the best cases, teachers are invited into the conversation about why and how learning walk data will be gathered, and the data is tailored to what teachers want and need as they grow in the profession. Learning walks are also an essential tool for the principal and coach to gather data on the real-time effectiveness of their action steps.

To make learning walks meaningful, we recommend taking a collaborative, transparent approach. Begin by scheduling classroom visits so that partners can visit the same rooms at the same times, and provide time for debriefing and reflection. Use the learning walk planning template in figure 3.4 to create your schedule, clarify the purpose of the visits, and determine the data that you will collect. After creating a learning walk schedule, let those teachers know when and why you are coming to their classrooms and what data you will collect while there. This step is important because it removes the element of surprise and helps teachers see the learning walk process as supportive rather than evaluative. When multiple people walk into a classroom unexpectedly, it can be daunting. Clear communication prevents this feeling.

Before learning walks: To ensure you and your partner are visiting teachers meaningfully, spend five to ten minutes discussing the following questions before you complete learning walks with your partner or individually.

- What teachers do we need to visit and why?
- What data will we collect? What are the look-fors?
- How will we use the data?
- What feedback is needed? How will we follow up with the teachers?
- How might this impact our coaching?

Figure 3.4: *Learning walk planning template.*
Visit ***go.SolutionTree.com/leadership*** *for a free reproducible version of this figure.*

After learning walks, debrief to compare observations, identify trends, and determine next steps.

At our school, this systematic approach to learning walks has reframed what teachers once perceived as *gotcha* moments into opportunities to connect classroom practice to schoolwide priorities. Clearly communicating our shared goals and our data-collection process ensures that the teachers see all our work as interconnected and our time as well spent in the pursuit of our collective goals.

After visiting a classroom, the principal and coach can use the learning walk reflection template in figure 3.5 (page 64) to reflect on what they observed and set clear next steps. Potential next steps may include deciding who will follow up with the teacher or what specific feedback they will provide.

After learning walks: To ensure you and your partner are visiting teachers meaningfully, spend five to ten minutes discussing the following questions after you complete learning walks with your partner or individually.

- What look-fors did we observe?
- Were there any look-fors that we did not observe?
- What are our next steps?

Figure 3.5: *Learning walk reflection template.*
Visit ***go.SolutionTree.com/leadership*** *for a free reproducible version of this figure.*

Turning Data Into Decisions

Once they have collected the data, partners need time and a protocol to dig in and diagnose. While results will vary from one partnership to another, there are really just two eventualities: (1) You didn't meet your goal—now what? or (2) You met your goal—now what? The *now what?* part can either stymie partnerships or galvanize them. We have found that intentionality is critical and makes the difference between successfully pursuing our goals and becoming sidetracked by distractions.

To maintain this intentionality, partners should schedule specific dates for reflection and adjustments as part of the partnership plan. These reflection and adjustment meetings give partners dedicated time to analyze data, consider progress, and measure the effectiveness of their collaborative actions. Figure 3.6 shows how partners might complete the action step reflection worksheet, which is a simple and systematic tool that lets them document progress, celebrations, and next steps. A simple organizational tool like this keeps meetings on track and goals at the forefront of conversations.

To illustrate this idea, consider our earlier SMART goal focused on improving reading comprehension through annotation and close reading. Partners might

Coaching Goal: By the end of the school year, 100 percent of our priority collaborative teams will meet their SMART goal.

Action Step	Progress	Celebrations	Next Steps
Plan professional development for SMART goal creation.	Completed	It went well! Teams created uniform SMART goals.	Lunch is interfering with our fifth-period facilitator meeting, so we must revisit our plan.
Support collaborative teams with SMART goal creation.	Completed	The top five and bottom five skills were listed in facilitator announcements. Coaches successfully facilitated conversations.	English and Algebra I teachers are implementing a new curriculum. How do we not overwhelm these teachers?
Provide feedback on SMART goals.	Completed	Coaches successfully facilitated conversations.	The principal and coach did not look at SMART goals together this month. We need a plan to avoid this in the future.

Figure 3.6: *Sample action step reflection worksheet.*
*Visit **go.SolutionTree.com/leadership** for a free reproducible version of this figure.*

review student work at a scheduled reflection point. The student work data may show that annotations are improving but that students are still struggling to apply the learning to their written responses. The partners can then use this evidence to determine next steps. Partners would document these decisions in figure 3.6, along with notes on the action step's progress and a plan for celebrating growth.

Whether analyzing classroom data, as in the literacy example, or reviewing collaborative team goals, the process remains the same. Partners rely on evidence to drive decisions, track progress, and commit to next steps.

Harnessing the Power of Reflection

The adult learning that comes from formative data analysis is the real product of this process. Educators must have time, space, and a protocol for the reflective work that yields insights into their next steps in order for them to learn and grow. To mount an effective response to *now what?*, the partnership framework must embed reflective practices for the partners, individual teachers, and teacher teams. In a healthy learning environment, the principal and coach set a standard that they must be transparent about their progress and willing to adapt to the direction indicated by the data analysis.

As Richard DuFour and Michael Fullan (2013) remind us, "a fundamental task of leadership at all levels in systemic reform is to create the conditions that allow people to be successful at what they are being asked to do" (p. 51). Our work as principal-coach partners relies on reflecting to ensure we are having the intended impact. We spend time at each principal-coach meeting being transparent about our work and efforts to meet our goals. Sometimes, we must admit our failings to one another and be honest about the time we didn't spend working with teachers or the commitments we failed to meet. Because we have established norms for how we treat one another during our meeting time, the space is safe. We can speak vulnerably about our challenges and receive feedback from our partners without becoming defensive. We do not engage in reflection for the sake of reflection, but we use our learning as an impetus for the creation of next steps. By reflecting together and generating next steps as a team, we are best able to hold one another accountable for the work of continuous improvement and ensure that our plans come to fruition, rather than falling victim to time and the commitment creep that plagues so many school leaders, despite their best intentions.

To make this work in your own setting, consider these steps.

1. Be transparent and vulnerable when reflecting on the impact of your work.
2. Focus on productive next steps rather than assigning blame for missed opportunities.
3. Determine and document next steps (see figure 3.6, page 65).
4. Hold yourself and your partner accountable for your commitments to each other and the work.

Use the monthly reflection template in figure 3.7 as a guide in this reflection process.

Before-Meeting Action	Spend ten minutes reflecting on the instructional focus question.
During-Meeting Actions	Each partner will have two minutes to share their celebrations. After each partner has shared, identify a focus for the next month.
Instructional Focus: • What should we celebrate? • What am I wondering about? • What are the upcoming commitments? • What is the focus of next month's meeting?	

Figure 3.7: *Monthly reflection template.*

Visit ***go.SolutionTree.com/leadership*** *for a free reproducible version of this figure.*

The Partnership Perspective

PRINCIPAL AND COACH INSIGHTS

PRINCIPAL PERSPECTIVE: *Rebecca*

As a principal, I realized that telling people what to do had limited impact, so I began trying to listen more and talk less. I wanted to ensure that all shareholders, especially teachers, had access whenever they needed something. I was committed to providing resources, including my time, to make sure teachers felt valued and included in our school community. It felt like a virtuous goal, and I congratulated myself for creating a place where all ideas were welcome and all initiatives had equal opportunity. However, I soon realized that saying yes to everything left me depleted of the time and focus that I needed to commit to the truly critical components of our school's mission and vision. The partnership I had created with Michelle and Brittany was critical to restoring my focus and helping me establish structure and boundaries for my time and energy. I realized that committing to too many new things was counterproductive; doing everything meant that I was doing nothing particularly well. Our time as principal-coach partners helps me intentionally allocate time for what truly matters. Additionally, it allows me to be clear with teachers about who we are as a school and what we value as a learning community.

Researcher and storyteller Brené Brown (2018) posits that "clear is kind," and I have come to rely on this maxim whenever I feel compelled to say yes to something that isn't in line with our school's priorities.

When we clearly communicate what we are doing and why we are doing it, shareholders are better able to understand why some things are not part of our plan, even if they seem to be worthy and interesting pursuits. I've learned that sometimes saying no ensures we have the time and space to do our work as a PLC committed to ensuring learning for all.

COACH PERSPECTIVE: *Michelle*

When asked about the most challenging part of my job as an instructional coach, I used to give a surface-level answer, like managing different personalities and time constraints. While that challenge is real, I've realized the actual difficulty lies in something deeper: ensuring that each day, I spend my time in meaningful and impactful ways. With constant distractions like meetings and endless emails, it is easy to lose sight of our instructional goals. The real challenge is creating a system of checks and balances to intentionally prioritize high-leverage coaching activities that make a difference.

Working with Brittany has been instrumental in refining my approach. Informal conversations while we were doing hall or cafeteria duty evolved into structured, intentional debriefing sessions. Together, we began auditing how we spent our days, asking ourselves tough but necessary questions: Was this activity the best use of our time? How did it contribute to teacher growth or student success? Was it aligned with our goals as coaches?

These reflective practices became ways to recalibrate when competing demands pulled us off track. We didn't just rely on instinct; we deliberately examined the impact of our choices, making adjustments to ensure our efforts were aligned with what mattered most. Our coaching conversations now center on being intentional and strategic to best support our teachers.

Through this process, I've learned that recommitting to high-leverage coaching activities isn't a one-time decision; it's a continuous practice. It requires ongoing reflection, collaboration, and, sometimes, the willingness to say no to good opportunities so you can say yes to the best ones. That intentionality has made me a better coach and, ultimately, helped me make a more significant impact in my school.

Partners Maintain Momentum

Let's revisit Coach Patel for a moment. The idea of holding people accountable used to make her pretty nervous. In her mind, ensuring accountability required confronting people who didn't meet expectations, and she was definitely not a fan of confrontation. She also feared that holding teachers and teams accountable would damage her relationships with them, and they would be less inclined to approach her as a coach. Principal Harvey, on the other hand, has no problem holding people accountable for clear contractual obligations. He lets teachers know his expectations for things like arriving at work on time and contacting parents when a student is failing. When they don't do those things, he recognizes that it is his responsibility to follow through with sanctions or discipline. However, he has no idea how best to respond when teachers or teams exhibit dysfunction in executing their shared goals. He gets really frustrated when teachers don't use formative assessment data or collaborate well with one another, but it's not like he can write them up for these failings. Principal Harvey and Coach Patel need a different way to embrace and communicate accountability for this work. They will find that their greatest leverage with teachers and teams is to respond to dysfunction with systemic, high-impact coaching moves.

All the educators we know work very hard each day, and it can be frustrating for them to realize when this work has not produced the desired results. We best honor the work of our partnership, teachers, and teacher teams by first acknowledging effort and assuming the best intentions. The important thing for the partners is not that they get everything exactly right all the time but that they keep moving forward. As a team, we commit to progress over perfection and do not let ourselves abandon our plans when we hit speed bumps on the journey. We extend this grace to one another and our teachers and teacher teams, feeling confident that we can hold teams accountable for their commitments in the same way that we hold each other accountable for ours.

That consideration extends to responding effectively to team dysfunctions and ensuring accountability through clear communication.

Responding to Team Dysfunctions

Our work is challenging, and having partners means that the lure of commiseration is strong. Commiseration can bind people together and help them unite against a shared enemy, but we have found that commiseration is actually the enemy of productive follow-through on our shared goals. To prevent our meetings from descending into mutual complaining sessions, we have established a protocol where we systematically respond to the challenges of our work by focusing on the high-leverage coaching activity that will help us best mitigate the dysfunction that slows us down.

While every dysfunction may feel unique to the time, the place, and the people who experience it, the reality is that many situations share a common antecedent and can be approached with a consistent response. Consider the following list of dysfunctions we see recur across teams and schools. The dysfunction response planner in figure 3.8 is an example of how we help one another refocus on our partnership when it veers off track, ensuring we address challenges in a way that strengthens our commitment to our shared goals.

The best principal-coach partnership accountability structures reinforce the interdependence of the partners by ensuring that both their positional authority and their strengths as instructional leaders are brought to bear when they're dealing with teacher and team dysfunction. If a teacher or team refuses to carry out a task, that is the principal's purview. If a teacher is trying something new and wants a set of nonevaluative eyes on their plans, it is probably best for the principal to allow the coach to take the lead.

Ensuring Accountability Through Clear Communication

Early in our time as principal and coaches, we often made commitments about the time we would spend together and the work we would do, usually early in the school year when hope springs eternal. We began the year with a ton of enthusiasm and the best of intentions, but as "required" parts of our jobs crowded in, we sacrificed our partnership time to any and all distractions. Because we were so familiar and comfortable with one another, we were probably *too* comfortable canceling meetings and putting off plans because we knew all would be forgiven. A shift occurred when we started to share our collective commitments with the larger school community. Once teachers and teams knew about the work to which we had committed ourselves and could see their roles in achieving our shared goals, it became much more difficult to cancel a meeting or scrap an initiative.

This shared understanding of the partners' work is critical to maintaining momentum throughout the year. It is one thing to cancel a meeting between partners but entirely another to cancel an initiative that involves and engages the entire school community in its improvement efforts. To ensure that you and your partner hold yourselves accountable for your commitments, publish your meeting times and agenda. Have a standing report-out section in a larger leadership team meeting. Invite your supervisor to join your meeting, and lay out your short- and long-term goals. Proudly publish the results of your work in your school and in community-facing communications. When your plan is public and widely known, you will be forced to be more consistent in meeting your commitments to your partner and the work.

Dysfunction	Partnership Actions to Consider
The partners do not meet regularly.	• Create a virtual calendar invite so that both the principal and the coach are notified about the meeting twenty-four to forty-eight hours in advance. • Find a day midweek to have a working lunch as a team. • Revisit how frequently the partners need to meet. If meeting every week does not seem sustainable, consider meeting every other week.
Partner norms were set in August but have not been addressed since then.	• Include norms on all agendas and review them at the beginning of every meeting. • Revisit the discussion tool for establishing norms (figure 1.1, page 15) and reestablish norms for the meeting. • Identify the norms that are not being followed, and have a quick critical conversation about why the norms are needed for a productive meeting.
In meetings, the partners are distracted and not actively listening.	• Consider using a single device during the meeting, which a designated partner will use to project the documents. • Use meeting time to practice your coaching skills; set a goal for each partner to paraphrase at least three times during the meeting. • Consider meeting in a new location that offers fewer distractions.
Goals and action steps were initially set but have never been revisited.	• Commit to using the action step reflection worksheet (figure 3.6, page 65) at least once a month during meetings. • If using a digital agenda, include a link to the partnership plan worksheet (figures 2.5, page 42, and 2.6, page 44) so you access the plan at each meeting. • As partners, choose one action step for the week, and include it at the top of your to-do lists, even the sticky note to-do list. At the end of the week, take five minutes (such as during hallway or lunchroom duty) to check on how the action step is going.
Decisions are based on opinion, not data.	• Collect data related to upcoming decisions (student performance data, classroom observation data, survey data, and so on). • During meetings, ensure a team member asks, "What evidence supports this decision?"
The partners tend to focus on future plans without taking the time to reflect on past experiences.	• Commit to using the monthly reflection template (figure 3.7, page 67). • At the end of each meeting, make a point of establishing the agenda for the next meeting. Include time on the agenda for reflection.

Figure 3.8: *Sample dysfunction response planner.*

Visit ***go.SolutionTree.com/leadership*** *for a free reproducible version of this figure.*

Principal-coach partners must also clearly communicate the partnership plan's accountability structures so that the teachers and teams with whom they are working understand the systematic process through which they intend to meet the school's instructional challenges. For example, partners who intend to monitor the SMART goals of teacher teams will do well to tell each team when their data will be reviewed and what interim feedback they will receive. If teachers are to be held accountable for implementing literacy strategies, the partners should inform them of the why, how, and when. If learning walks will be the mode of data collection for any initiative, teachers should have the opportunity to view the tool and receive timely data as feedback. Clear communication is the key to ensuring that the commitments of the principal-coach partners become the collective commitments of the school community.

Calibration Conversations

The calibration conversations for this phase give you an opportunity to reflect on challenges in monitoring your work as a team. Whether you are struggling to find time to meet or to identify the actions that will have the biggest impact on school-improvement initiatives, this activity encourages you to examine how your current practices support your efforts. Each scenario highlights how partners might sometimes lose their way. Read each scenario and imagine it playing out in your own context. How would you react if this were your partnership? Use the read, react, and reflect protocol in figure 3.9 to compare your own practices to those in the scenarios and identify ways to strengthen your work together.

Protocol	1. Determine the partnership's progress for each scenario as it relates to: • Prioritizing coaching • Measuring what matters • Maintaining momentum 2. Discuss the potential next step for this partnership.
Scenario 1	Whenever a new email arrives from the district lead for academics, Principal Harvey forwards it to Coach Patel. He knows he is sending mixed messages by flooding her inbox with tasks, but he doesn't know to whom else he would delegate them. These tasks need to be done, and he knows that if they are on her list, he can mentally cross them off his. Coach Patel has asked to meet with him about her schedule, and he is willing to do it if he can find the time to have a meeting.

Scenario 2	The principal-coach partnership is back on track. Principal Harvey and Coach Patel have audited their time and ensured that they have been clear with each other and with school shareholders about their commitments. They are monitoring data that speaks to their partnership goals and have determined that some teams are meeting their goals and others are not. At this point, the partners have a new challenge: Their original plan doesn't include the next steps, and they don't know how to provide feedback that helps teams move forward. Now what?
Scenario 3	Coach Patel is satisfied with meeting some of the interim goals of the partnership plan. She and Principal Harvey have recommitted to their action steps and spent more time working with teachers. However, as the school year goes on, they notice that some teacher teams have lost momentum. As the end of the semester nears, everyone knows that the school days will be characterized by frequent schedule changes and students will be distracted. In fact, the principal-coach partners seem distracted too. They had plans to finish strong, but maybe they should just put things on hold until the schedule calms down a little. Still, yesterday, the head of the English department approached Coach Patel and wanted to know why she has not conducted any learning walks lately. It was embarrassing to admit that she just hasn't had the time.

Figure 3.9: *Read, react, and reflect protocol.*

Final Thoughts

Phase 3 of the partnership framework aims to help partners stay the course through some of the most challenging parts of the school year, when the optimism and energy of a team's initial commitments may wane and the myriad demands of team members' roles distract them from what they envisioned in phase 1. In this sense, this phase is when it is most critical for partners to be intentional about how they spend their time and how they communicate with each other and the school's shareholders. Everyone intends to follow through with their commitments when they are making them, but systems ensure that they have the structures and support to do so. We have found that the best systems are simple, and the best way to communicate with each other is with frankness and transparency. The tools presented in this phase are easily adaptable to all school environments and can track efforts and ensure accountability for the simplest to the most complex plans. Tracking your action steps and reflecting on your progress are not revolutionary. Still, when done with fidelity and approached with a learning mindset, they can empower principals and coaches and transform a school into an instructionally focused community of learners.

When working with your partner, consider the actions listed in figure 3.10. Complete each action in the checklist to ensure you fully implement phase 3.

- ☐ Conduct an instructional time audit (figure 3.1, page 57).
- ☐ Reflect on and discuss any coaching shifts (figure 3.2, page 58).
- ☐ Identify distractions and monitor your commitments (figure 3.3, page 61).
- ☐ Plan your learning walks as an extension of your accountability communication (figure 3.4, page 63).
- ☐ Reflect on your learning walks (figure 3.5, page 64).
- ☐ Reflect on your action steps and identify celebrations and next steps (figure 3.6, page 65).
- ☐ Celebrate wins and identify a monthly focus to maintain momentum (figure 3.7, page 67).
- ☐ Create systematic responses to any common dysfunctions (figure 3.8, page 71).
- ☐ With your partner, work through the read, react, and reflect protocol for phase 3 (figure 3.9, page 72).

Figure 3.10: *Phase 3 checklist—Monitoring and adjusting.*

Visit ***go.SolutionTree.com/leadership*** *for a free reproducible version of this figure.*

Pause to Reflect

Reflect on the following questions as you close out phase 3.

- What structures do you currently have to prioritize coaching, measure what matters, and maintain momentum?
- What tools does your team need to start using to monitor its work and adjust its actions?

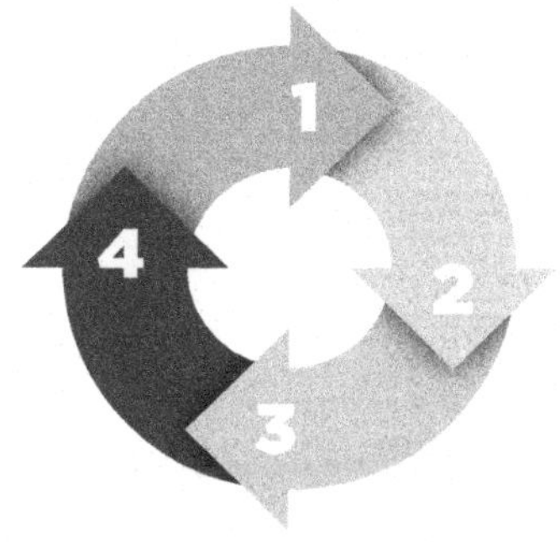

PHASE 4

Looking Ahead

- Sustain the work through the analysis of data.
- Celebrate successes and capitalize on wins.
- Build the foundation for future success through careful planning and allocation of resources.

Consider the following hypothetical scenario.

Principal Strong and Coach Lee have worked on their partnership throughout the school year, doing their best to avoid distractions and be intentional about their time together. Their roles have become increasingly interdependent as they have worked toward their shared goals. As they approach the last phase of their partnership plan, they know they need to gather summative data on their work and celebrate the school's progress. They are also exhausted, having carried much of the load. They now find themselves in the season of the school year when everything seems to happen all at once. School budgets are due, and so are district-mandated professional development plans. Required testing will upend school-day schedules, and students are increasingly testing the boundaries of the school's behavioral expectations. There are also events—so many events! Dances, concerts, school plays, and regional sports tournaments fill every spare spot on the school calendar, stealing the time and focus that kept the partnership on track. And then there are the siren calls of new initiatives. The emails and fancy flyers that show up on their desks offer opportunities for staff to attend conferences, hear from professional speakers, or learn about new technology that will "transform" the school. If Principal Strong and Coach Lee do not make purposeful choices now, they risk losing all the momentum they established throughout the implementation of their partnership plan.

Reflection Questions

Based on the preceding scenario, answer the following questions.

- How do you ensure that you finish strong when it comes to analyzing your plan's summative data?
- How do you embed celebrations for your wins and capitalize on your successes?
- How can you continue to widely disperse leadership to increase the collective lift of the school's mission and vision?
- How do you stay the course when the newness of your work wears off and you are faced with increasing demands on your time and attention?
- How do you work with your partner to make critical decisions about school logistics (staffing, budgeting, professional learning priorities, and so on)?

Principal Strong needs an instructional coach to help her navigate the path forward. Coach Lee must have a voice in the decisions that allocate the school's resources to ensure a coherent plan moving forward. It's make-or-break time for this partnership. By being intentional about their moves in phase 4, these partners can ensure that their hard work up to this point propels them to greater clarity and coherence in their vision of learning for all.

Here, we'll explore the fourth phase of the partnership framework, where partners turn their attention to sustaining what they've built. Partners can accomplish this by providing targeted support, maintaining focus, celebrating wins, and identifying and replicating best practices.

Collaboration in Action: Key Moves and Essential Tools

The fourth phase of the partnership framework is designed to help principal-coach partners finish strong and move forward after a full cycle of the partnership plan. To do this, they need to (1) sustain the work through the analysis of data, (2) celebrate successes and capitalize on wins, and (3) build the foundation for future success through careful planning and allocation of resources.

Partners Sustain the Work Through the Analysis of Data

To sustain the efforts of their partnership plan during times of transition, partners must focus on data that helps them evaluate the progress they have made. Partners will need to analyze qualitative and quantitative data that clearly shows how their plan has borne out their intentions. Additionally, they must evaluate which aspects of the plan are worth continuing, which initiatives have mixed results, and which ideas should be abandoned despite their initial appeal. For the partners who have faithfully followed their plan, SMART goals have guided their action steps and will determine whether they have been successful. SMART goal success can function as a summative assessment of their shared goals. The SMART goal analysis protocol in figure 4.1 can help the partners gather their thoughts and document their learning from the SMART goals they have set for the year.

Step 1: Review Your Team's SMART Goal	
Step 2: Analyze the Data	
Consider Quantitative Data Results Consider assessment scores, learning walk trends, teacher and student attendance rates, and student engagement metrics.	**Notes:**
Consider Qualitative Data Results Consider teacher and student reflections, collaborative team conversations, and classroom observations.	**Notes:**
Compare the Results to Baseline Data Consider improvements or trends that have emerged since you began this work.	**Notes:**
Step 3: Determine Impact	
Identify Success Indicators Identify what is working well. Which strategies had the most significant impact?	**Notes:**
Examine Mixed Results Where did we find inconsistencies? What challenges did we face?	**Notes:**

Figure 4.1: *SMART goal analysis protocol.*

continued →

Explore Missed Targets What didn't work as intended? What barriers can we identify that hindered our success?	**Notes:**
Reflect on Lessons Learned What did we learn through this process? How did this work make us better?	**Notes:**
Step 4: Decide on Next Steps	
Commit to Continue What should be sustained based on our results?	**Notes:**
Commit to Support What do we need to adjust for significant impact?	**Notes:**
Choose to Abandon What should we discontinue due to lack of effectiveness?	**Notes:**
Commit to Grow What do we need to learn more about? What resources or professional development might we engage with to facilitate this learning?	**Notes:**

Visit ***go.SolutionTree.com/leadership*** *for a free reproducible version of this figure.*

Of course, even if a team has not met its SMART goals, there is much to be learned from the data gathered around the team's efforts. An important part of any data analysis is to examine the gaps: For whom was the work least successful? What factors mitigated an individual's or team's success? Teacher interviews and feedback are critical sources of data, and if the school leadership has provided a safe place for teacher voice, that feedback can be instrumental in widely dispersing leadership for the collective lift of whole-school improvement. The same vulnerability that served the principal and coach as they established their norms will now serve them as they seek the information they need to improve their practice.

DuFour and Fullan (2013) remind us:

> Building the capacity of educators to meet the challenges they face requires a servant-leader mindset. A sink-or-swim philosophy

> does not build capacity; too many people drown. A "we hope people will figure it out" approach does not build capacity. Hope may be a virtue, but it is not a strategy. (p. 51)

Moving from hope to strategic intervention requires a systemic response from the principal-coach partnership.

Providing Targeted Support

Once the partners have identified areas of concern, they need to purposefully plan for targeted support based on performance levels and feedback. Not every challenge will merit, or even benefit from, the same response. Targeted support must be:

- Based on data, not assumptions
- Aligned to support specific gaps, not generalized interventions
- Customized to fit the needs of the teacher or teacher team

When the principal and coach meet to discuss how to provide targeted support, considering each teacher team individually is helpful. We suggest using the targeted support planning tool in figure 4.2 (page 80) to begin developing a robust support plan.

Maintaining Focus

The distractions that the principal and coach have navigated all school year may seem to multiply as the year draws to a close. Even schools that operate on a nontraditional schedule can feel the pressure as students transition from one session to the next or when new students matriculate. It can be tempting to write off a school year, even when school is still in session, as planning for the future can be more appealing than dealing with the messy, conflicting pulls of the present moment. While phase 4 encourages partners to look toward the next iteration of their plans, just like in previous phases, the interdependent principal and coach must hold each other accountable for completing the cycle of action to which they committed themselves in phase 1. Once again, being intentional about their time together can help them refocus when distractions abound.

At this phase, the challenge is less about setting direction and more about sustaining focus. The step-by-step structures established in previous phases are what keep the principal and coach grounded in their commitments. Ideally, phases 1–3 have followed DuFour and Fullan's (2013) recommendation for long-term planning: "The long journey must be broken down into immediate, doable steps. Vague generalities must be redefined into specific indicators to clarify how people throughout the organization can monitor their progress" (p. 66). Careful meeting

Step 1: Assessing the Support Needed for Teachers and Teacher Teams

Using the provided descriptions, identify where teachers or teacher teams fall in the *reinforcement*, *refinement*, or *redirection* support categories. Choose specific strategies from the suggested actions to plan your next steps.

Type of Support	Purpose	Targeted Teachers and Teams	Actions to Consider
Reinforcement	Sustain, strengthen, and replicate best practices across the school.	Teachers and teacher teams who are meeting or exceeding expectations	☐ Share best practices. ☐ Facilitate peer coaching. ☐ Celebrate progress. ☐ Provide immediate, positive feedback.
Refinement	Provide feedback and coaching to increase instructional effectiveness.	Teachers and teacher teams who are showing partial or inconsistent progress toward expectations	☐ Discuss potential barriers to progress. ☐ Provide differentiated professional learning opportunities (recorded lessons, co-teaching, lesson studies, peer learning walks, and so on). ☐ Conduct frequent learning walks paired with constructive feedback that is specific, actionable, and focused on areas of improvement. ☐ Have coaching conversations focused on reflection through the use of open-ended questions and active listening.
Redirection	Reestablish expectations and provide direct intervention.	Teachers and teacher teams who are significantly struggling to meet expectations	☐ Conduct interviews to determine obstacles. ☐ Provide a one-on-one coaching support plan, including specific feedback. ☐ Create clear, actionable short-term goals. ☐ Emphasize expectations and the positive impact they will have.

Step 2: Planning Next Steps

Complete the chart to create a targeted support implementation plan for each teacher and teacher team you identify.

Teacher or Teacher Team Name	Reinforcement, Refinement, or Redirection	Specific Actions Planned	Person Responsible	Implementation Timeline	Monitoring, Reflection, and Adjustments
Mr. Hunt	Refinement	Schedule four learning walks that include feedback that is specific, actionable, and focused on classroom management.	Ms. Mozingo	Two weeks	The teacher is still expressing a need for support with his sixth-period class. The coach will continue the coaching cycle with the teacher.
Ms. Wilson	Reinforcement	Coordinate with the teacher to set dates for specific learning walks when trying a new literacy strategy and follow up with a short check-in after each learning walk.	Ms. Marrillia	Two weeks	Ms. Wilson will share a strategy with the collaborative team at the next meeting and invite teammates to observe her classroom if interested.
Mr. Christian	Redirection	Schedule a facilitator check-in to plan the agenda for collaborative team meetings and review how to facilitate a data analysis protocol before the next data analysis session.	Ms. Marrillia	Three weeks	The facilitator is feeling more confident planning agendas for team meetings, but the collaborative team continues to struggle with bringing data to those meetings.

Figure 4.2: *Targeted support planning tool.*

Visit ***go.SolutionTree.com/leadership*** *for a free reproducible version of this figure.*

planning and agenda creation can ensure that partners have the structures they need to finish strong.

The principal and coach may audit past agendas at least once during this phase. This process allows partners to assess meeting frequency and focus, determine whether agendas align with the team's SMART goals, and check progress on action steps. The principal and coach can then look for topics that dominate too much time or goals that have been neglected. This process also provides evidence to celebrate wins or make final adjustments before the end of the school year. The agenda-auditing tool in figure 4.3 can facilitate this reflection.

Directions: With your partner, review the last four or five meeting agendas and respond to the following prompts.

Here's What	
What do the agendas reveal about the partnership's productivity? • *Agendas show that the last four meetings have focused on planning professional development.* • *Only one agenda shows evidence of reviewing learning walk data.* • *Productivity seems strong for planning upcoming professional development but less strong for analyzing data and reflecting.*	What do the agendas reveal about the partnership's commitment to a shared SMART goal? • *We are committed to planning meaningful professional development for teachers, but we have not prioritized looking at learning walk data and responding with coaching and feedback.*
So What?	**Now What?**
What does this data reveal about the partnership's commitment to collaboration and instructional priorities? • *Our planning activities overshadow instructional priorities.* • *We seem to be more focused on designing the professional development than using the data to plan for coaching and feedback.*	What are our next steps to maintain momentum? • *We will commit to completing one period of learning walks together so that we can calibrate feedback.* • *We will commit to dedicating at least one agenda item each week to examining learning walk data.*

Source: Adapted from Marrillia, 2021.

Figure 4.3: *Agenda-auditing tool.*

Partners Celebrate Successes and Capitalize on Wins

Besides recognizing the distractions that could cause them to falter at the finish line, the principal-coach partners must recognize that morale often lags when people are tired. Celebration is an essential practice that allows a school to reinvigorate staff who may be desperately looking forward to a break or are burned out by their multiplying responsibilities. Richard DuFour, Rebecca DuFour, Robert Eaker, Mike Mattos, and Anthony Muhammad (2021) remind those working to transform their schools that "it is not merely achieving small victories but recognizing those victories and the people behind them that sustains momentum for change" (pp. 321–322). Celebrations build trust, shore up confidence, and inspire effort. Muhammad (2018) recounts:

> The positive school cultures I observed constantly celebrated the things the school valued. These celebrations were both planned (or institutionalized) and impromptu, and all were authentic. Recognition was genuine and not manufactured for the sake of giving the appearance of false appreciation in the midst of low productivity. These schools set clear expectations for all stakeholders—students, teachers, administrators, support staff, and parents. When these expectations were met, the achievements were celebrated proudly and publicly. (p. 126)

As with all things, intentionality is key to embedding celebration as part of your strategic plan.

Celebration should be an integral part of each phase of the partnership framework, but phase 4 is aptly poised for larger celebrations that showcase the school's successes. Celebrations can and should take many forms. Different teachers and teams will feel honored by different approaches, and celebrations should be as differentiated as the coaching plan has been. Educator and author Marc Johnson (2015) asserts that principals must "be accessible to teams, differentiate support to teams, monitor the achievement of goals, and celebrate success" (p. 26). Some teachers will be most gratified by public recognition for their efforts. These individuals feel comfortable with ceremonies, social media posts, and announcements over the intercom. Other teachers or teams may respond better to rewards or incentives. They may appreciate a lunch provided by the parent or alumni association or enjoy a gift of books or teacher supplies. Other teachers and teams may feel most honored when their work is showcased or when they are asked to share best practices and show off their best stuff to other educators.

As the principal-coach partners build capacity within the school, they should also offer opportunities for growth as celebrations. Educators Jeanne Spiller and Karen Power (2022) urge schools to celebrate growth, which "requires leaders to have an intentional awareness of cultural shifts as they happen and then bring attention to the efforts that guide the changes" (p. 101). Tapping teachers and teams for professional development opportunities like learning conferences, book studies, and shadowing opportunities lets these educators know that their principal and coach have faith in them and see their potential to extend their learning and grow in the profession.

To avoid generic praise and acknowledgment and ensure that all educators are celebrated, you must consider how they each impact your school. Do you have an innovative teacher who is always looking for new strategies to try with their classes? Do you have an administrator who regularly anticipates challenges and proactively plans ways to avoid issues? Is there an athletic coach who monitors grades weekly to ensure that their players are seeing success in the classroom and on the field? Have you noticed a teacher team that is always the first to respond with student work samples when requested? Innovators, problem solvers, encouragers, and rule followers all impact school goals and should be recognized for their unique impact.

As you and your partner consider ways to celebrate the educators in your building, use the intentionality with celebrations matrix in figure 4.4 to differentiate your celebrations so that you honor the educators and their work specifically.

Celebrations are easy to put at the bottom of your to-do list, so it is imperative that the coach and principal make celebrations a priority. Make it a challenge to celebrate at least one or two staff members or teams per week, whether you do that through writing positive notes, leaving specific feedback, or providing lunch. Celebrating small wins allows you to scale the success of your partnership work throughout the larger school community.

Scaling Success

After they've collected and analyzed the data and honored the hard work of successful teachers and teams, partners must consider how to scale the success of individuals and teams to the larger school community. Researchers Andrew J. Milat, Adrian Bauman, and Sally Redman (2015) find that "effective scaling up requires the systematic use of evidence, and it is essential that data from implementation monitoring is linked to decision making throughout the scaling-up process." The partnership framework asks that partners use the formative data they have gathered throughout the implementation process and the summative data they have

Type of Educator	Observable Actions	Ways to Celebrate
Innovators These educators are always trying new strategies and striving for innovation within the classroom and school.	• They use a new strategy in class, in a meeting, or during professional development. • They share a new idea in a meeting or during professional development. • They integrate new technology in class, in a meeting, during professional development, or in a schoolwide system. • They plan for differentiated instruction. • They design a project that allows students to be creative, collaborate, and solve problems. • They use multiple methods of assessment within a unit.	• Send an email to the educator with a picture or video of students or teachers engaging with the new strategy or idea and highlight the impact. • Acknowledge the creativity and innovation through a positive note. • Provide feedback on how the new strategy or idea had an impact and contributed to learning. • Provide specific examples of innovation during evaluations. • Share the new strategy or idea with the school through an email, announcement, or newsletter. • Encourage or make ways for the educator to attend or lead professional development. • Institute an Innovator of the Month award.
Problem Solvers These educators are curious and always eager to find solutions to problems.	• They identify a challenge and implement a solution to address it effectively. • They include others to help find solutions to challenges or problems. • They anticipate a challenge and proactively plan ways to avoid it. • They help a colleague address and find solutions to problems. • They participate in a schoolwide committee that addresses a specific issue.	• When leaving feedback, be sure to include specific data that connects to a challenge or goal they may be working on. • Write a positive note that highlights the specific ways the educator's critical thinking and problem solving have had an impact. • Buy the educator a book that they might enjoy, and include a note emphasizing their positive impact. • Provide specific examples of problem-solving skills during evaluations. • Provide opportunities for the educator to be a mentor. • Publicly acknowledge the educator's accomplishment at a faculty meeting or in a schoolwide email. • Encourage or make ways for the educator to attend or lead professional development. • Institute a Problem Solver of the Month award.

Figure 4.4: *Intentionality with celebrations matrix.*

continued →

Type of Educator	Observable Actions	Ways to Celebrate
Encouragers These educators are always looking to encourage people and increase their sense of belonging.	• They create a positive and safe learning environment where every voice is heard. • They monitor student learning and adjust instruction to meet learning needs. • They celebrate student success. • They continually offer praise for effort, growth, and accomplishments. • They provide scaffolds so that all students find success. • They provide and create opportunities for student voice and choice. • They attend schoolwide events outside the school day.	• Include positive reinforcement when leaving feedback. • Write a positive note that highlights the specific ways the educator has helped increase a sense of belonging at school. • Provide specific examples of encouragement during evaluations. • Collect a set of thank-you notes written by students or other teachers for the teacher. • Institute an Encourager of the Month award.
Rule Followers These educators always rise to challenges and will follow through with whatever is asked of them.	• When asked to try a new strategy, they use the strategy within a week. • They always have data ready at team meetings. • They actively participate in team meetings and professional development. • They provide student work samples for documentation. • They behave as a team player during new initiatives. • They exhibit near-perfect attendance.	• Send an email to the educator thanking them for their commitment and follow-through. • Write a positive note that highlights the specific ways the educator's dependability has had an impact. • Provide specific examples of reliability during evaluations. • Give the educator a small gift that includes planning supplies (sticky notes, pens, agendas, and so on). • Highlight the teacher who is having an impact on current initiatives at a faculty meeting or in a schoolwide email. • Honor the teacher with near-perfect attendance via a positive note or a shout-out in a morning email. • Institute a Rule Follower of the Month award.

Visit ***go.SolutionTree.com/leadership*** *for a free reproducible version of this figure.*

analyzed at the end of the SMART goal terms to make informed decisions about moving forward. This data is an essential tool as they scale their successes to the larger school community. At least some of the data used to scale successes should be qualitative in nature; let teachers and teams who have been successful offer their testimonials and share their lessons learned.

We have found that teachers can have an incredible influence on their peers, and allowing them to share their success stories helps create a community of learners who rely on one another as they attempt new strategies and engage in action research. We use the process shown in figure 4.5 to ask teachers to reflect on their work and share their experiences with one another, across content areas and teams. This helps us disseminate best practices in a way that feels organic to our mission and creates a sense of ownership and pride for those educators who are learning together.

Directions: We are so grateful for your leadership as a teacher leader, and we would love to hear your thoughts about our work this school year. Please prepare a brief reflection (three to five minutes) on the key lessons learned.

Step 1: Reflection (Before the Meeting)

Identify one success, one challenge, and one next step you are taking based on your learning. Frame your reflection using the success, challenge, and growth framework.

- **Success:** What worked well? (What was something that you did as a team or as a leader that had a direct, positive impact on student learning?)
- **Challenge:** What was difficult? (Was there a specific barrier that impacted your ability to reach your goal?)
- **Growth:** What's next? (As a team or team leader, what would you like to learn more about?)

The following components of your role may serve as starting points for your reflection.

- Facilitating and managing time during team meetings
- Communicating with team members
- Setting goals and action steps
- Resolving conflicts within the team
- Creating assessments or engaging in data analysis
- Planning for interventions and extensions
- Mentoring new teachers
- Planning and leading professional development

Figure 4.5: *Teacher leader share session.*

continued →

Step 2: Structured Share (During the Meeting)

Each teacher leader will share using the success, challenge, and growth framework. During this time, colleagues should do the following.

1. Colleagues will silently listen and jot down key takeaways, questions, or connections. (Two minutes)
2. Participants will ask only clarifying questions to ensure understanding. (Two minutes)
3. Participants will share the following. (Three minutes)
    - "I appreciate . . ." (Highlight a strength or insight.)
    - "I wonder . . ." (Pose a reflective question.)
    - "You might try . . ." (Offer a constructive suggestion.)

In addition to scaling successes, partnerships must abandon failed initiatives if they hope to capitalize on their wins.

Abandoning Failed Initiatives

Throughout phase 4, the partners should ask themselves, "What can we replicate?" and also honestly ask themselves, "What do we need to abandon?" Communication will be key to creating a coherent vision of the school's improvement trajectory. The stop-doing list is ultimately as important as the to-do list, as it frees up the time and resources for successful initiatives. However, if principals and coaches do not clearly communicate to their shareholders why they have stopped doing something, those decisions can seem capricious and may sow distrust and reluctance to try new things when people don't understand why previous efforts have been abandoned.

The list of things we have stopped doing in the fifteen years we have worked together could fill its own book. There have even been moments when we have wistfully recalled an abandoned practice and asked each other, "Now, why did we stop doing that?" The keys to creating a coherent approach are intentionally vetting decisions, using data to ensure we can support our moves, scaling up our successes, and setting aside initiatives that do not serve our shared goals. The keep, stop, and start reflection activity in figure 4.6 can help teams purposefully allocate their time and energy and articulate the reasoning behind their decisions that impact the learning environment.

The number of required reports that land in a principal's inbox could fill their own book. You might feel like Principal Strong when you're contemplating the paperwork required by district and state or provincial entities, which involves submitting multiple plans and reports intended to hold schools accountable for external mandates.

Directions: Identify the task, process, or behavior you want to reflect on or improve. Consider your ideas and sort them into the following categories.

- **Keep:** What is currently working and should continue?
  - *Collaborative team meetings are centered on student learning rather than logistics.*
  - *Collaborative teams are using common formative assessments.*
  - *Learning walks are consistent and aligned with instructional priorities.*
- **Stop:** What current actions are unproductive or outdated and should stop?
  - *Collaborative teams are spending too much time creating supplemental resources.*
  - *Agenda items are not consistently aligned to essential standards and curriculum work.*
- **Start:** What new actions will help us achieve our goal?
  - *We should increase the use of data analysis protocols to adjust instructional practices when needed.*
  - *We should build teacher capacity with instructional routines and strategies that support student learning.*
- **Reflection:** Choose one or two focus items from your list. Create a list of doable action steps in the space provided.
  - *Provide coaching to individual teachers and teacher teams on how to adapt curriculum for learners struggling to show mastery of essential standards.*
  - *Provide facilitators with training and coaching on implementing a data analysis protocol.*

Figure 4.6: *Keep, stop, and start reflection activity.*

Visit ***go.SolutionTree.com/leadership*** *for a free reproducible version of this figure.*

Planning for Professional Learning

Principal Strong regards the district email about her required "professional learning plan" with trepidation. With its all-caps deadlines and red directives, it seems intimidating and removed from her and her coach's work throughout the year. She is tempted to fill out required templates and shove them in a folder somewhere while she gets on with running the school. Coach Lee, however, sees the plan as an opportunity and urges her to approach the task with the same mindset they have brought to their local commitments. If they work together and involve the school's shareholders, the formalized professional learning plan can function as a launchpad for the next cycle of the partnership plan. It can reflect the shared goals of the partners and detail the efforts they will take to ensure learning for all.

Effective principal-coach partnerships are always engaged in the process of planning, implementing, evaluating, and reflecting on the professional learning of the educators in their school. Phase 4 is unique in that it often falls at the time of year when schools have to document their yearlong commitments to professional learning in a formal way. While every school calendar is different, schools often must submit a professional learning plan for external accountability. To ensure yearlong planning, many of these plans are due at the end of a school year to inform the next year's allocation of time and resources. As with all external accountability measures, it may be tempting to treat this plan as a compliance activity—something to check off a to-do list and then shelve until the due date rolls around next year. However, principal-coach partners can and should integrate the creation of this plan into their work to synthesize it with their partnership plan and ensure that resources are appropriately allocated. A school's annual professional learning planning is an opportunity to publicly and financially commit to initiatives that will continue and to explore new learning that can move the school closer to its goal of learning for all.

In drafting a professional learning plan, partners should use the reflective documents that have guided their work throughout the year, revisiting their agendas and reflective protocols that have captured their successes and frustrations during each phase. They should ask themselves what is working and what needs to be tweaked. They should seek out teachers' perspectives to ensure they capture all learning elements as they make decisions about moving forward. While most required documentation has elements that serve district or larger priorities, we urge schools to work within these confines to document their local priorities and commitments as well. The professional learning planning document in figure 4.7 can make this work actionable and aligned with the professional learning that the partners envision.

Directions: Use this document to ensure you have considered the foundational elements of professional learning planning. It will help you align your process with your school's mission and instructional vision as well as student learning priorities.

Key Elements to Consider Before Professional Learning Planning

Are we creating a space for all shareholders to be involved in meaningful collaboration? Yes / No

Are we ensuring that our professional learning goals are aligned with schoolwide priorities and district goals? Yes / No

Do we have a process for defining the roles and responsibilities of all participants? Yes / No

Are there opportunities to assess progress and adjust practices as needed? Yes / No

Components of the Professional Learning Planning Process	
What is the mission of our school?	*We are a positive and purposeful learning community dedicated to ensuring high levels of learning for all.*
What is the purpose of our professional learning? How will it improve student learning and teacher practice?	*We will increase the use of literacy strategies across all content areas so that students engage with rigorous texts, improve their writing, and expand their use of disciplinary vocabulary.*
What are the primary goals of professional learning?	• *We will ensure all teachers routinely use at least two literacy strategies throughout the year.* • *We will increase student achievement in reading and writing.*
How will shareholders be engaged in the process (collaborative teams, faculty meetings, or embedded professional learning)?	• *Collaborative teams will plan how to embed literacy strategies in their content area.* • *Faculty meetings will be used to celebrate progress and introduce new literacy strategies.* • *Embedded professional learning will include learning walks followed by coaching conversations.*
Who will plan, implement, and evaluate the professional learning?	*The principal and instructional coaches will oversee implementation and accountability for the components of professional learning.*
What are the timelines?	• *August to September: Whole-school professional development will occur during monthly faculty meetings.* • *October to December: Collaborative teams will plan for literacy strategies and reflect on implementation.* • *January to March: Collaborative teams will continue to embed literacy strategies in their planning. Coaching cycles will be implemented with individual teachers.*
What resources will we use to support the work?	*Teams will use professional texts and videos, the literacy plan, benchmark assessments, and other student learning data.*
When and how will we reflect on the effectiveness of the professional learning?	*The principal and coach will schedule meetings in September, December, March, and May to reflect on effectiveness. The partners will use benchmark assessment data, teacher feedback, learning walk data, and formative assessment data to measure progress.*

Figure 4.7: *Professional learning planning document.*

*Visit **go.SolutionTree.com/leadership** for a free reproducible version of this figure.*

Professional learning plans usually include multiple components of learning for all staff. It is important that principals and coaches prioritize their own professional development as part of their larger professional learning plans. They can easily get caught up in taking care of the needs of the school community, but in the same spirit as airlines urge passengers to secure their own oxygen masks before assisting others, principals and coaches need to seek out and secure their own professional learning as they are planning for their school's trajectory. The professional learning for the principal and coach should speak directly to their shared goals and should be tied to the SMART goals that inform their success. Coaches specifically should be able to seek out and receive professional learning opportunities specific to their role. Educator, speaker, and consultant Courtney Tate (2024) explains why: "For most schools and districts, there is no formal professional development plan or course, although it's crucial that coaches receive thorough training to deepen their knowledge of teaching practices." Once again, the principal is critical in ensuring this work can happen. Tate (2024) notes, "School leaders play a pivotal role in ensuring that instructional coaches receive ongoing relevant and directly applicable training for their daily responsibilities."

The Partnership Perspective

PRINCIPAL AND COACH INSIGHTS

PRINCIPAL PERSPECTIVE: *Rebecca*

My best-laid plans and early-September enthusiasm are often no match for the principal panic that sets in around March. I am guilty of descending into survival mode when commitments start to pile up, and my calendar feels overwhelming. Like at many schools, our springtime activities consist of testing, testing, and more testing, and the disruption to regular school-day routines means that our coaching meeting time often is sacrificed to the demands of proctoring state assessments and maintaining behavioral expectations in our hallways and cafeteria. I feel guilty sitting down and shutting the door to have meaningful conversations with my coach when the busy world is whirling outside. By maintaining our regular meeting time, however, we ensure that this time of year is as important to our success as the early days when all our efforts look shiny and new. The systems we establish early on hold the line against my principal panic and keep me engaged in the process until the finish line.

COACH PERSPECTIVE: Brittany

In my first years as a coach, I took pride in being the go-to for every teacher. I even won the Helping Hand award at our staff holiday party, which felt like a badge of honor for being the ultimate team player. I was the technology expert, the classroom management consultant, the strategy queen, and even the keeper of the supply closet key. I could run a copier like nobody's business. At first, I thought this was what it meant to be a great coach—to be helpful, to be available, and to have all the answers.

But over time, the role began to feel unsustainable. I realized that I was unintentionally creating a dependency on meeting everyone's needs. Was I building teachers' capacity or caught in a loop of helping rather than empowering them? I started to see that answering every question makes life easier for teachers. I wanted to support and build relationships, but I was rushing around to save the day, which wasn't aligned with my ultimate goal: to elevate teaching and learning.

It was pivotal when Michelle reminded me, "You don't need all the answers. Focus on asking the right questions and helping teachers find their own answers." That simple reminder shifted my focus. I realized coaching was not about being the expert on every topic but about helping teachers develop expertise and confidence. The shift from helper to coach wasn't immediate, but with time, I saw the value in moving from quick fixes to meaningful, capacity-building conversations. Creating these relationships is key to finishing strong and ensuring we end with the same energy with which we begin. When our time and attention are stretched by competing demands, the collective expertise in which we have invested throughout the year ensures that we hold one another accountable for our shared commitments to student and adult learning.

Partners Build the Foundation for Future Success Through Careful Planning and Allocation of Resources

As the partnership plan enters the final phase, partners must take the time to build the foundation for future success. In a practical sense, this means aligning the school's budget and resources with the priorities the partnership has established. School budgets are big, unwieldy things that require the input of multiple shareholders who are beholden to myriad restrictions and rules. Savvy partners understand that only so much can be spent in any direction, and oftentimes, investing in quality professional learning can feel like a luxury. American Association of School Administrators policy analyst Noelle Ellerson (n.d.) concludes:

> School budgets allow districts to translate sometimes intangible missions, operations and objectives into reality by outlining and providing specific programs and funding/financial terms. A school budget helps bridge the gap that can exist between a district's stated goals and resource allocation. The budget process forces the discussion that will inform choices among various programs competing for the limited available resources. (p. 2)

Careful allocation of the school's budget will ensure that staffing, scheduling, and outside initiatives are appropriately resourced to meet the school's needs and reach the plan's goals.

Staffing

Money is not the only resource that your school needs to allocate to pursue worthy goals. You must use time and staff in ways that best maximize the impact of these finite and precious resources. As you and your partner contemplate staffing shifts or changes at the end of a school cycle, it is critical that you are:

- Preserving your coach's time
- Assigning staff to roles that best serve their expertise and your students
- Building capacity within your current staff to amplify your improvement efforts moving forward

Intentionality with staffing is especially important as the teacher shortage across the United States becomes more pronounced. According to researchers at the Learning Policy Institute, "Estimates [for the year 2024] indicate that, at a minimum, 406,964 positions were either unfilled or filled by teachers not fully certified for their assignments, representing about 1 in 8 of all teaching positions nationally" (Tan, Arellano, & Patrick, 2024). The pressure to put a certified teacher in front of every student can pull coaches back into classrooms, where they cover classes and fill in at a moment's notice when substitute teachers don't show up.

Throughout this text, we have urged principals and coaches to be strategic about where a coach spends their time and to consider how they can empower other staff members to support the effort. Nowhere is this more important than in phase 4. At this point, a coach can multiply their impact by empowering teacher leaders to take greater responsibility for guiding their teams. This includes finding creative ways to extend professional learning through collaboration and ongoing instructional growth. School staffing specialist Cheryl Hoover (2024) states:

> Implementing a strategic staffing model that embeds collaboration might be one of the best ways to use the talents of teachers while providing valuable instructional supports for inexperienced educators, such as uncertified teachers, beginning teachers, resident teachers in grow your own programs, and student teachers.

To scale any improvement efforts, partners also have to build capacity, and that can happen only once they have aligned the school's resources with the mission and vision of their work. Principal-coach partners spent part of phase 2 building collective capacity by empowering teachers to lead. Here is where those efforts come to fruition as the partners take stock of the talents and potential of the human capital in the building and position those resources in pursuit of continued improvement.

Scheduling

School schedules allocate the most precious resource: time. Schedule creation should be subject to the same consideration as any other finite school resource, with teams asking themselves how to spend their time to ensure they are supporting their shared goals. If the principal or coach is not the person who creates the master schedule, they still share the responsibility to ensure that the schedule reflects the mission and vision of the school. You should consider the following when it comes to creating the master schedule.

- Educators need time to work together. This time should be frequent and built within regular work hours.
- Productivity is impacted by the time of day when teachers meet. If all meetings happen after a long day of teaching, teachers may be less likely to enthusiastically collaborate.
- You may need to rethink whole-faculty time to create common meeting time for critical teams. It's possible that much of the messaging of a traditional faculty meeting can be disseminated in other ways.

Educator Alison Hamacher (2024) asserts that "with careful planning and collaboration, school schedules can be optimized to support student growth and development while also promoting teacher collaboration and empowerment." The school that has committed to collaborative work time for its staff must reflect that commitment in its schedule. Hamacher (2024) believes that "seamless scheduling for shared staff can lead to a more coherent learning experience for students, which in turn produces better student outcomes."

For some schools, this can mean ensuring common planning time for teacher teams, which is a practice that has served us well. At the beginning of our school's improvement journey, our teacher teams met once a week after school, during our district's contractual meeting time. However, that meant all our teams were meeting at once, and the coach and principal could participate in a limited number of team meetings in any given week. Creating common planning time during the day was critical to ensuring our coach and principal were able to join these teams on a regular basis, and it solidified our commitment to this collaborative work. It certainly meant more logistics to figure out for our master schedule, but ensuring that our time allocation aligned with our instructional priorities allowed us to build capacity with our teacher leaders and teams. Regardless of how your school chooses to craft a master schedule, it must allocate time as intentionally as it allocates other resources, and it must make that commitment visible, in concrete terms, to all shareholders.

Incorporating Outside Initiatives

State, provincial, and district initiatives can change each year, and with those changes come mandates for individual schools, often whether they like it or not. The partners must find ways to create coherence in the work they are asking of teachers and teams and make connections between varying, sometimes competing, interests. When contemplating the prospect of incorporating outside initiatives, you must do the following.

- Consider how the initiatives might support or detract from the current work of the school.
- Communicate transparently with all shareholders regarding the why and how of the implementation.
- Regularly monitor the impact of new initiatives on the plan and overall school environment.

Curriculum and instruction specialist Nancy Latham (2017) explains, "This concept of strategic coherence is especially important in the school context, because schools are frequently awash in the latest reform ideas, and are often implementing several reforms at once." We committed to working as a PLC in 2010, but in that time, we have had to incorporate new programs, state-mandated curriculum changes, infusions of capital to try new things, and an influx of multilingual learners, who have required us to think about teaching and learning in new ways. We have been challenged to integrate new ideas and initiatives with the processes and structures that we believe work best, and to communicate to staff how these strands are woven into the existing fabric of our school. If the principal and coach do not lead the conversation when change occurs, teachers may very quickly assume that the new initiative is just another thing, and that it will soon pass.

To create credibility, the principal-coach partnership must, once again, proceed with intentionality in both resource allocation and communication. The reality of modern schooling is that a school may not have complete autonomy for making decisions about the initiatives it enacts. According to researchers at the Public Education Leadership Project at Harvard University (n.d.), "Putting a district-wide strategy into practice requires building a coherent organization that connects to teachers' work in classrooms and enables people at all levels to carry out their part of the strategy." The principal and coach must ensure that they communicate a unified vision for the school's professional learning and convey the importance of each aspect of the work that contributes to realizing the school's mission.

Calibration Conversations

The fourth phase of the partnership framework is an intentional time of reflecting and planning to ensure continuous improvement. At the end of this phase, we invite you to consider scenarios that explore how you might implement the work or sometimes lose your way. Read each scenario and imagine it playing out in your own context. How would you react if this were your partnership? Use the read, react, and reflect protocol in figure 4.8 to compare your own practices to those in the scenarios and identify ways to strengthen your work together.

Protocol	1. Determine the partnership's progress for each scenario as it relates to: • Sustaining the work through the analysis of data • Celebrating successes and capitalizing on wins • Building the foundation for future success through careful planning and allocation of resources 2. Discuss the potential next step for this partnership.
Scenario 1	Principal Strong regards her end-of-year calendar with some measure of dread. Every school day has some program or interruption, and every evening has some event that requires her attendance. She had felt so good about the progress that she and Coach Lee were making, but now, she is just happy to get through the school day. The summer break may let her catch her breath, but until then, her meetings with her coach are on hold because of her packed calendar. She's pretty sure that the stuff they tried this year has been successful, and the formative data seems to bear that out, so she figures she will keep things exactly the same next year. Why mess with a good thing?

Figure 4.8: *Read, react, and reflect protocol.*

continued →

Scenario 2	Celebrations are Coach Lee's favorite things. He loves to plan all the details for each event and loves the looks on the faces of the participants as they beam with pride over their accomplishments. This year, he is excited to plan even bigger celebrations highlighting the data that speaks to the school's success. He knows he wants to include everyone in the events, but not everyone succeeded this year. He isn't sure how to navigate the situation or get teachers talking about their success with one another in a way that doesn't hurt people's feelings. Principal Strong has not been much help lately, as she is so busy with other things. He may have to figure this out for himself.
Scenario 3	Principal Strong and Coach Lee have finally allocated time to meet and plan for their next steps. They are divided, however, on how to proceed. Principal Strong is super excited to attend a few conferences during their break and wants to try out many new strategies next year. Coach Lee thinks that their plates are already full and that they should just keep doing what they are doing, as it has mostly worked out. They arrive at a stalemate just as the district-required professional development deadline arrives. They don't know how to draft a new plan, much less allocate resources to fund what they want to do. They seem to have forgotten how to work together at a critical juncture where their collaborative approach is more important than ever.

Final Thoughts

As a team, we have been guilty of looking for the next shiny thing, abandoning an initiative before we have properly analyzed the data that speaks to whether it succeeded. We have also been guilty of looking at unmet SMART goals and declaring the goals themselves suspect, rather than the action steps that failed to produce the desired effects. We have failed to celebrate our successes or properly recognize the efforts of our teachers and teams as they embraced change. We have allowed ourselves to be swept along by the current of busyness, make excuses, and beg off meeting when the hectic pace of the day waylaid our plans to work together. We have done so many things that could have led us off course or caused us to lose faith in one another or the process. Luckily, however, we have figured out ways of coming back together and holding one another accountable for our shared goals.

So much of our work now reflects the lessons we have learned by failing at things, and so much of our success is attributable to the interdependence of our partnership. We have learned by doing and certainly learned by failing, and it is the interdependence of our partnership that allows us to continue the work with energy and optimism. By creating the systems that keep our principal-coach partnership focused, we have been able to stay the course, even when circumstances and resources change and challenge us.

When working with your partner, consider the actions listed in figure 4.9. Complete each action in the checklist to ensure you fully implement phase 4.

- ☐ Conduct a SMART goal analysis (figure 4.1, page 77).
- ☐ Plan for targeted support (figure 4.2, page 80).
- ☐ Audit your team's agenda (figure 4.3, page 82).
- ☐ Celebrate with intention (figure 4.4, page 85).
- ☐ Empower teachers to share their testimonies (figure 4.5, page 87).
- ☐ Review your instructional priorities (figure 4.6, page 89).
- ☐ Reflect on current professional learning opportunities (figure 4.7, page 90).
- ☐ With your partner, work through the read, react, and reflect protocol for phase 4 (figure 4.8, page 97).

Figure 4.9: *Phase 4 checklist—Looking ahead.*

Visit ***go.SolutionTree.com/leadership*** *for a free reproducible version of this figure.*

Pause to Reflect

Reflect on the following questions as you close out phase 4.

- How does your team sustain the work through the analysis of data?
- What structures do you currently have to celebrate successes and capitalize on wins?
- What tools does your team need to start using to foster future growth?

EPILOGUE

Modern schooling is a complex amalgamation of varying demands, interests, and initiatives. However, despite the noise of our modern age, the purpose of school remains unchanged from eras past. Schools exist so students can learn what they need to know to live in the world and create the best futures for themselves. When school leaders and coaches can commit to this relatively simple mission, their work has the capacity to cut through some of the distractions that beset school leaders and stymie coaches' best intentions when it comes to learning. We wrote this book for two reasons.

1. To clarify the work we do, even to ourselves, as we continue to navigate challenges
2. To inspire principals and coaches to harness the power of their collaboration and gain the capacity and expertise to best leverage their roles in the school

We have been forthcoming about all the ways that we have stumbled on our journey as a principal and coaches, and we have acknowledged the frustrations that may cause teams to lose their way. Nobody undertakes this journey without stumbling over obstacles or without becoming distracted by all the noise and motion in a school. We assert that these challenges can often be blessings in disguise, and working through them grants your team the opportunity to become something greater than its individual members.

As current practitioners, we know that we must continue to learn, just as we ask our students to learn. We need to confront the changing world and the changing population with an action-research perspective and the optimism that, by sharing our journey and empowering others to learn with us, we are building capacity to carry on our mission, even amid change. We are not the same people we were when we met one another years ago, and we don't necessarily inhabit the same roles, but we maintain trust in one another and in the interdependence of our roles. Christopher E. Trombly (2014), dean of the College of Education at Southern Connecticut State University, who has researched complexity in modern schooling, states:

> Genuine change in schools requires that educators—administrators and teachers, alike—are prompted by reform efforts to work ever more closely with one another around issues of improved instruction, constantly learning from and continually providing feedback to one another, until ongoing reflection upon and refinement of new instructional practices replace the systems' former patterns of behavior. (pp. 47–48)

Throughout the writing of this book, we had to confront processes that no longer served us and abandon some things that had become routine. The exciting part, however, came as we created new solutions and fine-tuned the tools and systems that help us work better. We urge you to use the tools that work for you; see appendix A (page 105) for examples. If these don't work for you, we encourage you to create your own tools that serve your partnership as needed and to continually revise the systems that keep you and your partner on track.

Regardless of what kind of principal or coach you are, you have the power to transform the trajectory of your school. We acknowledge that we have been incredibly fortunate to work with one another, and we know that sometimes we can be our own greatest fans, but any partners can find ways to work together, even if they don't have an existing relationship, or they have wildly different personalities or ways of working in the school. The processes we have presented can help any team work toward greater efficiency and effectiveness and may help partners uncover gifts in themselves and in each other that they didn't realize they had.

Although this book is demarcated by four phases that generally align with the seasons of a traditional school year, we urge you to take stock of your current reality, regardless of the season or situation, and commit to building a relationship that helps you better understand your role and your power to influence change. If you do nothing else as a result of reading this, we hope you develop a vision of how your team could function and a commitment to take the first next step. Maybe you and your partner will finally take the time to schedule standing meetings with each other or sit down to establish norms for your time together. Maybe you have established trust and created the time and space to meet, but you need to get concrete about your shared goals and the action steps you will take to meet them. Maybe you have done much of the work of phases 1 and 2, but you need to build capacity within the school to scale your efforts to a wider audience. Maybe you just need to take the time to acknowledge all that your school has done to ensure student learning, and you will plan a celebration that inspires your lead learners to continue the charge. Wherever you are on the journey, we want you to know that we have been there too, usually more than once. For each phase you embrace, your path will evolve and often loop back on itself as your students, faculty, community, and partnership change along with it.

There is no one way to be a powerful team, but all teams benefit from a shared mission and vision and a powerful commitment to one another. We work as partners not because we are required to do so but simply because there is no way we could do the work alone. We lean on one another when we are distracted, discouraged, and out of ideas. We celebrate one another when we succeed, and our individual successes are shared victories—not because we are the same person but because we are working on the same goal. Our journey keeps us committed to our school and one another because we truly believe in the power of our shared work. We wish you and your partner the best as you move forward together, lean on each other, and learn together as you pursue the noble mission of the school you serve.

APPENDIX A

The Partnership Framework Alignment Guide

This partnership framework alignment guide connects the key moves of each phase of the framework to essential tools and guiding questions. As your partnership continues to develop, use this guide to focus your attention and resources on the greatest levers for change associated with each framework key move.

	Key Moves	Essential Tools	Guiding Questions
	Phase 1: Setting the Stage for Collaboration		
1	Partners establish norms.	• Sample discussion tool for establishing norms (figure 1.1, page 15)	• How do we build trust?
2	Partners clarify roles and responsibilities.	• Sample identifying roles and responsibilities tool (figure 1.2, page 17) • Example discussion tool for instructional leadership roles (figure 1.3, page 20)	• How do our roles complement each other in this work? • Where are there opportunities for us to collaborate?
3	Partners create clarity regarding the partnership.	• Meeting planner template (figure 1.4, page 21) • Tools for setting priorities (figures 1.5, page 22, and 1.6, page 22)	• When will we meet? • What are our coaching priorities?
4	Partners hold each other accountable.	• Sample meeting agenda (figure 1.7, page 23)	• How will we hold each other accountable for ensuring priorities?

continued →

	Key Moves	Essential Tools	Guiding Questions
Phase 2: Establishing Goals and Actions			
5	Partners write shared instructional goals.	• Tools for establishing a shared instructional SMART goal (figures 2.1, page 31, and 2.2, page 32)	• What are we trying to accomplish as a partnership?
6	Partners create a partnership plan.	• Partnership plan data-vetting tools (figures 2.3, page 36, and 2.4, page 36) • Partnership plan worksheets (figures 2.5, page 42, and 2.6, page 44)	• Based on our shared goal, what are our action steps? How will data inform our progress?
7	Partners build capacity to empower teacher leaders.	• Building teacher and team capacity reflection tool (figure 2.7, page 49)	• How are we currently building team and teacher capacity?
Phase 3: Monitoring and Adjusting			
8	Partners prioritize coaching.	• Sample instructional time audit tool (figure 3.1, page 57) • Coaching shift considerations (figure 3.2, page 58) • Commitment creep analysis tool (figure 3.3, page 61)	• Do our calendars reflect our priorities? • How do we maximize our time and impact? • What activities are distracting us from our priorities?
9	Partners measure what matters.	• Learning walk planning template (figure 3.4, page 63) • Learning walk reflection template (figure 3.5, page 64) • Sample action step reflection worksheet (figure 3.6, page 65) • Monthly reflection template (figure 3.7, page 67)	• How do learning walks play a role in the partnership plan? • We didn't meet our goal—now what? • We met our goal—now what? • How do we establish a reflection routine?
10	Partners maintain momentum.	• Sample dysfunction response planner (figure 3.8, page 71)	• How do we respond to partnership dysfunctions?

Phase 4: Looking Ahead			
11	Partners sustain the work.	• SMART goal analysis protocol (figure 4.1, page 77) • Targeted support planning tool (figure 4.2, page 80) • Agenda-auditing tool (figure 4.3, page 82)	• How did we do on our shared SMART goal? • For whom was the work least successful? • What factors mitigated an individual's or team's success? • What do our agendas reveal about our work?
12	Partners celebrate successes and capitalize on wins.	• Intentionality with celebrations matrix (figure 4.4, page 85) • Teacher leader share session (figure 4.5, page 87) • Keep, stop, and start reflection activity (figure 4.6, page 89) • Professional learning planning document (figure 4.7, page 90)	• How will we intentionally celebrate the work that is being done? • How will we use teacher perspectives to plan next steps? • What can we replicate? What do we need to abandon? • How do we plan for future professional learning?

APPENDIX B

Partnership Calendars

Planning is key to a successful partnership. Partnership calendars help partners map their work across the week, month, and year. Use these tools to track your progress, stay focused on shared goals, and remain productive throughout the school year. We recommend taking a few minutes at each meeting to update the calendars so that they reflect current priorities, completed action steps, and upcoming commitments.

Year at a Glance

Directions: Create a calendar that displays all the months of the year at a glance. Circle your current phase and identify any major events or significant deadlines (professional development days, testing windows, school-improvement plan due dates, and so on).

Month: Phase: 1 2 3 4 Events: Deadlines:	Month: Phase: 1 2 3 4 Events: Deadlines:	Month: Phase: 1 2 3 4 Events: Deadlines:
Month: Phase: 1 2 3 4 Events: Deadlines:	Month: Phase: 1 2 3 4 Events: Deadlines:	Month: Phase: 1 2 3 4 Events: Deadlines:
Month: Phase: 1 2 3 4 Events: Deadlines:	Month: Phase: 1 2 3 4 Events: Deadlines:	Month: Phase: 1 2 3 4 Events: Deadlines:
Month: Phase: 1 2 3 4 Events: Deadlines:	Month: Phase: 1 2 3 4 Events: Deadlines:	Month: Phase: 1 2 3 4 Events: Deadlines:

Monthly Calendar

Directions: Fill in the calendar with important dates and action steps. Review it weekly to stay on track. At the end of the month, review what you have accomplished and note any unfinished action steps or tasks to carry over to the next month.

Things to plan for include the following.

- Principal-coach meetings
- Learning walks
- Professional development
- Major events and deadlines
- Celebrations

Month:				
Phase:	**Goal:**	**Action Steps:**		
Monday	**Tuesday**	**Wednesday**	**Thursday**	**Friday**

Weekly Planning and Reflection

Directions: Include actions, meetings, deadlines, and tasks for each day of the week. Highlight your priorities.

Week:	
Action Steps to Focus on This Week:	
Monday	
Tuesday	
Wednesday	
Thursday	
Friday	
Action Step Progress:	
Celebration of the Week:	
Next Week's Focus:	

REFERENCES AND RESOURCES

Anderson, V., & Wallin, P. (2018). Instructional coaching: Enhancing instructional leadership in schools. *National Teacher Education Journal, 11*(2), 53–59.

Bahrami, Z., Heidari, A., & Cranney, J. (2022). Applying SMART goal intervention leads to greater goal attainment, need satisfaction and positive affect. *International Journal of Mental Health Promotion, 24*(6), 869–882. https://doi.org/10.32604/ijmhp.2022.018954

Brown, B. (2018, October 15). *Clear is kind. Unclear is unkind* [Blog post]. Accessed at https://brenebrown.com/articles/2018/10/15/clear-is-kind-unclear-is-unkind on January 17, 2025.

Conzemius, A. E., & O'Neill, J. (2014). *The handbook for SMART school teams: Revitalizing best practices for collaboration* (2nd ed.). Solution Tree Press.

Darling-Hammond, L., Hyler, M. E., & Gardner, M. (2017). *Effective teacher professional development.* Learning Policy Institute. Accessed at https://learningpolicyinstitute.org/sites/default/files/product-files/Effective_Teacher_Professional_Development_REPORT.pdf on September 23, 2025.

D'Auria, J. (2015). Learn to avoid or overcome leadership obstacles. *Phi Delta Kappan, 96*(5), 52–54.

Dirks, K. T., & de Jong, B. (2022). Trust within the workplace: A review of two waves of research and a glimpse of the third. *Annual Review of Organizational Psychology and Organizational Behavior, 9*, 247–276.

DuFour, R., DuFour, R., Eaker, R., Many, T. W., Mattos, M., & Muhammad, A. (2024). *Learning by doing: A handbook for Professional Learning Communities at Work* (4th ed.). Solution Tree Press.

DuFour, R., DuFour, R., Eaker, R., Mattos, M., & Muhammad, A. (2021). *Revisiting Professional Learning Communities at Work: Proven insights for sustained, substantive school improvement* (2nd ed.). Solution Tree Press.

DuFour, R., & Fullan, M. (2013). *Cultures built to last: Systemic PLCs at Work.* Solution Tree Press.

Ellerson, N. (n.d.). *School budgets 101.* American Association of School Administrators. Accessed at www.aasa.org/docs/default-source/resources/reports/school-budgets-101.pdf on February 14, 2025.

Ferriter, W. M. (2020). *The big book of tools for collaborative teams in a PLC at Work.* Solution Tree Press.

Frei, F. X., & Morriss, A. (2020, May–June). Begin with trust: The first step to becoming a genuinely empowering leader. *Harvard Business Review.* Accessed at https://hbr.org/2020/05/begin-with-trust on August 8, 2025.

Fullan, M. (2011). *The moral imperative realized.* Corwin.

Fullan, M., & Knight, J. (2011). Coaches as system leaders. *Educational Leadership, 69*(2), 50–53.

Fullan, M., & Quinn, J. (2016). *Coherence: The right drivers in action for schools, districts, and systems.* Corwin.

Fusarelli, L. D., & Fusarelli, B. C. (2018). Instructional supervision in an era of high-stakes accountability. In S. J. Zepeda & J. A. Ponticell (Eds.), *The Wiley handbook of educational supervision* (pp. 131–155). Wiley Blackwell.

Gillis, T. J. (2022). *School principals and instructional coaches: An examination of their working relationships in Maine schools* [Doctoral dissertation, University of Maine]. DigitalCommons@UMaine. https://digitalcommons.library.umaine.edu/etd/3650

Hamacher, A. (2024, April 16). *Best practices for school scheduling at middle and high schools* [Blog post]. Accessed at www.edficiency.com/post/best-practices-for-school-scheduling-at-middle-and-high-schools on February 15, 2025.

Hoover, C. (2024, October 1). *Strategic staffing models can increase instructional supports.* Texas Association of School Boards (TASB). Accessed at www.tasb.org/news-insights/strategic-staffing-models-can-increase-instructional-supports on February 11, 2025.

Horne, C., & Mollborn, S. (2020). Norms: An integrated framework. *Annual Review of Sociology, 46*, 467–487.

Ippolito, J., & Bean, R. M. (2019, November 1). A principal's guide to supporting instructional coaching. *Educational Leadership, 77*(3). Accessed at www.ascd.org/el/articles/a-principals-guide-to-supporting-instructional-coaching on September 23, 2025.

Johnson, J., Leibowitz, S., & Perret, K. (2017). *The coach approach to school leadership: Leading teachers to higher levels of effectiveness.* ASCD.

Johnson, M. (2015). *How to coach leadership in a PLC.* Solution Tree Press.

Killion, J., & Harrison, C. (2017). *Taking the lead: New roles for teachers and school-based coaches* (2nd ed.). Learning Forward.

Killion, J., Harrison, C., Bryan, C., & Clifton, H. (2012). *Coaching matters.* Learning Forward.

Knight, J. (2022). *The definitive guide to instructional coaching: Seven factors for success.* ASCD.

Knight, J. (2024, May 21). *Principal support: The key ingredient for successful instructional coaching* [Blog post]. Accessed at www.instructionalcoaching.com/principal-support-the-key-ingredient-for-successful-instructional-coaching on May 14, 2025.

Lambert, L. (2002, May 1). A framework for shared leadership. *Educational Leadership, 59*(8). Accessed at www.ascd.org/el/articles/a-framework-for-shared-leadership on September 23, 2025.

Latham, N. (2017, July 11). *Why the concept of strategic coherence is important for understanding implementation success* [Blog post]. Accessed at https://learningforaction.com/lfa-blogpost/strategic-coherence on February 11, 2025.

Lencioni, P. (2012). *The advantage: Why organizational health trumps everything else in business.* Jossey-Bass.

Lumpkin, A., Claxton, H., & Wilson, A. (2014). Key characteristics of teacher leaders in schools. *Administrative Issues Journal, 4*(2), 59–67.

Many, T. W., Maffoni, M. J., Sparks, S. K., & Thomas, T. F. (2018). *Amplify your impact: Coaching collaborative teams in PLCs at Work*. Solution Tree Press.

Marrillia, M. (2021). Giving all teachers the coach they deserve. In S. V. Kramer (Ed.), *Charting the course for leaders: Lessons from priority schools in a PLC at Work* (pp. 181–196). Solution Tree Press.

Matsumura, L. C., Garnier, H. E., & Resnick, L. B. (2010). Implementing literacy coaching: The role of school social resources. *Educational Evaluation and Policy Analysis, 32*(2), 249–272.

Matsumura, L. C., Sartoris, M., Bickel, D. D., & Garnier, H. E. (2009). Leadership for literacy coaching: The principal's role in launching a new coaching program. *Educational Administration Quarterly, 45*(5), 655–693.

Mayer, R. C., Davis, J. H., & Schoorman, F. D. (1995). An integrative model of organizational trust. *Academy of Management Review, 20*(3), 709–734.

McAdam, K. J. L. (2023). *Principal-instructional coach partnership: An exploration into the influence of trust* [Doctoral dissertation, University of Illinois Urbana-Champaign]. Illinois Digital Environment for Access to Learning and Scholarship (IDEALS). www.ideals.illinois.edu/items/127317

Milat, A. J., Bauman, A., & Redman, S. (2015). Narrative review of models and success factors for scaling up public health interventions. *Implementation Science, 10*, Article 113. https://doi.org/10.1186/s13012-015-0301-6

Muhammad, A. (2018). *Transforming school culture: How to overcome staff division* (2nd ed.). Solution Tree Press.

National Center for Education Statistics. (2023, October 17). *Most public schools face challenges in hiring teachers and other personnel entering the 2023–24 academic year* [Press release]. Accessed at https://nces.ed.gov/whatsnew/press_releases/10_17_2023.asp on March 1, 2025.

Pinheiro, G., & Alves, J. M. (2024). Educational teams: Building professional and organizational learning communities. *Frontiers in Education, 9*, Article 1446905. https://doi.org/10.3389/feduc.2024.1446905

Public Education Leadership Project at Harvard University. (n.d.). *PELP Coherence Framework*. Accessed at https://pelp.fas.harvard.edu/coherence-framework on February 11, 2025.

Schmoker, M. (2004). Learning communities at the crossroads: Toward the best schools we've ever had. *Phi Delta Kappan, 86*(1), 84–88.

Shen, J., Wu, H., Reeves, P., Zheng, Y., Ryan, L., & Anderson, D. (2020). The association between teacher leadership and student achievement: A meta-analysis. *Educational Research Review, 31*, Article 100357. https://doi.org/10.1016/j.edurev.2020.100357

Showers, B., & Joyce, B. (1996, March 1). The evolution of peer coaching. *Educational Leadership, 53*(6). Accessed at www.ascd.org/el/articles/the-evolution-of-peer-coaching on August 8, 2025.

Spiller, J., & Power, K. (2022). *Leading beyond intention: Six areas to deepen reflection and planning in your PLC at Work*. Solution Tree Press.

Tan, T. S., Arellano, I., & Patrick, S. K. (2024, July 31). *State teacher shortages 2024 update: Teaching positions left vacant or filled by teachers without full certification*. Learning Policy Institute. Accessed at https://learningpolicyinstitute.org/product/state-teacher-shortages-vacancy-2024 on May 15, 2025.

Tate, C. (2024, September 16). *How to plan effective professional development for instructional coaches*. Edutopia. Accessed at www.edutopia.org/article/effective-professional-development-instructional-coaches on February 11, 2025.

Trombly, C. E. (2014). Schools and complexity. *Complicity, 11*(2), 40–58.

West, L. (2017). Principal and coach as partners. *The Journal of Mathematical Behavior, 46*, 313–320. https://doi.org/10.1016/j.jmathb.2017.02.003

INDEX

S

T

V

W